D0299842

Epic Lifestyle

By
Sean Smith and Lloyd Zeigler

Unless otherwise noted, all scripture quotations are taken from the New King James
Version of the Bible. Copyright 1988 by International Bible Society.
Used by permission of Zondervan Publishing House. All rights reserved.

The "NKJV" trademark is registered in the United States Patent and Trademark Office by
International Bible Society.

Epic Lifestyle
ISBN: 0-9749892-2-3
2005 by Sean Smith Ministries
P.O. Box 2821
San Ramon, CA 94583
USA

Cover Design by Brian Orme
Typeset by Tri Vizion Media Group, Inc.
Edited by Stacy Lippert

Published by
Pointblank Publications
Sean Smith Ministries
www.seansmithministries.org
(925)829-0851

Printed in the United States of America.
All rights reserved under International Copyright Law. Contents and/or cover may not be repro-
duced in whole or in part in any form without the express written consent of the publisher.

Acknowledgements

Sean Smith:

To Barb, my wife and best friend, you've been my soul mate since you were in college. Your Godly example as a wife, mother, and partner in ministry has propelled me to further heights.

To Brandon and Brittany, you guys just keep amazing Daddy with the pure devotion and "crazy love" passion for Jesus that you both walk in, in your teenage year—give history a shove!

To Nina Walls, thanks for your example of persistence and good, old-fashioned hard work. You're the best mom any guy could have.

To Gaylord and Patti, thanks so much for your prayers and life-impartation to our family. You have truly modeled humility, wisdom, and self-sacrifice. Thanks for being spiritual parents to us.

To Mike and Michelle, once again you guys have poured out your blood, sweat, and tears, typing and managing this combo-book project. Thanks big time; you guys are still the bomb!

To Dee Davis, thanks for standing in the gap for our family and ministry. Only eternity can reveal all that you have meant to us and the kingdom.

To Mario Murillo, thanks for opening some doors as well as your offices to get us started in a significant phase of ministry and time in our lives. Your words have definitely impacted ministry for us.

To Donnie and Cindy Moore, thanks for your profound model of what it means to be an on fire disciple of Christ. Your lives have impacted many.

To Lloyd Ziegler, thanks for your amazing input in this project and for making time in your ever-demanding schedule. You are a tremendous friend, and your expertise and creativity are off the charts!

To Jesus—most of all, my precious Savior and Eternal King. You saved me, and my feeble attempt to say "thank you" is to extend that lifeline to my generation. I praise You for Your loving kindness and grace in my life.

Lloyd Zeigler:

Thanks to my Pastor, Tommy Barnett, who has inspired me to accomplish dreams, evangelize the world, and love people more than others think is practical.

To the MC Directors and Staff leaders who daily unlock the life potential of disciples by unveiling spiritual truth. God bless you as you make evangelists who prophetically share the only message that will allow you to live an epic lifestyle.

I could not have done this without my discipleship staff here at MC USA. Thanks for brainstorming with me, organizing notes, and typing. Your motivation and creative ideas are more than any leader could want.

Forward

The movie, "The Lord of the Rings," had just ended. Moved by the Holy Spirit my seventeen year old son, Jesse, walked to the front of the theater and began to preach Jesus to the entire auditorium. As he began to preach, a young woman whom he did not know fell to her knees and began to weep in intercession for the lost. Unbeknownst to Jesse, other young people stood at the doors of the exit and began to pray for the sick. Later on, Jesse overheard two older men speaking to one another and one remarked, "That was just what the Jesus Movement was like. They would preach anywhere and everywhere!"

Something is going on again. There are whispers of another Jesus Movement in the air. The late sixties and seventies witnessed an extraordinary spiritual awakening as tens of thousands of young people worldwide turned to Jesus. They said that you could have said, "Boo!" and people would have gotten saved. One friend of mine walked up to some "Jesus Freaks" and asked, "What time is it?" They replied, "It's time for you to get saved." And he did!

I hear the bones of revival rattling again as a new generation is pressing in to see their own move of God. Could this revival be the greatest awakening in America? For every revival there is a new restoration. The ancient harvesting tools are being rediscovered and a new evangelist takes to the streets again—it's the prophetic evangelist; it is you and me. Our harvesting tools are not primarily the sickle of gospel tracts, but the combine of revelation, risk, and resurrection power. The healing revival is moving from the church buildings into the streets.

Recently, a friend of mine dreamt one night that a young man stepped into the middle of the street and was struck by a car. Lying in the street hemorrhaging, the victim died. In the dream my friend laid his hands on the young man and prayed. Immediately the hemorrhaging stopped and the man was raised from the dead. The following day that dream actually happened! As the young man stepped out into the street, he was violently struck by a car. As he lay there hemorrhaging, my friend did what he had seen in his dream. He laid his hands on the young man and the hemorrhaging stopped immediately and he miraculously recovered! My friend had seen the will of God for that situation in a dream the night before. He took the risk of faith, prayed, and saw the heavenly plan manifested on the earth.

This is not an isolated story. Testimonies like this one are exploding all across the country and around the world. A "Revelation Generation" is taking the greatest prophetic evangelist, Jesus, to the streets again, and many are being drawn to Him. We are witnessing history (His-story) again. Jesus said to the woman at the well, "You have had five husbands and the one you are with is not yours." The woman's response was, "Lord, I perceive you are a prophet." She then went and proclaimed to her whole city, "Come, see a Man who told me all things that I ever did..." (John 4:17-42). Because of this experience, many in the city were saved.

My friend, Sean Smith, who carries the countenance and courage of Jesus, is one of the forerunners and equippers of this movement. In this book you will find valuable insights into what the great end-time harvest will look like. With the skill of a most serious student of Scripture, years of experience in personal and mass evangelism, Sean is creating a wake for the new breed of nameless and faceless evangelists who are emerging.

Sean shows us how to look beyond the natural into the spiritual realm to hear and see the secrets of a person's heart; you will also learn how to receive a word of healing for a person's body. Even now we are seeing just glimpses of this movement of power encounters, but just wait until it breaks out full-scale over a generation. Many men will look on in wonder and be drawn unto the Lord.

I am dreaming a dream with Sean Smith that the Healing Revival of the 1950's will look like a drop in the bucket of what is to come. Not just big time healers and massive tent revivals, but little people like you and me just "doing the stuff."

Read this book and find your own name written in it, for you are His workmanship in Christ Jesus to do good works.

Lou Engle,
Founder of The Cause USA,
Author of "Redigging the Wells"

Contents

Introduction

"The first demand any work of any art makes upon us is surrender. Look. Listen. Receive. Get yourself out of the way. (There is no good asking first whether the work before you deserves such surrender, for until you have surrendered you cannot possibly find out.)"
– *C.S. Lewis*

No true child of God can take any credit for a move of the Spirit any more than a fan can believe his cheers scored the winning points in a team's athletic contest. Who is paying whom?

I have been blessed to see an increase of emphasis on Spirit-driven soul-winning in recent days. Many have come to the forefront in prophetic evangelism. Prophetic evangelism is not only on the radar–it *is* the radar when it comes to the emerging harvest. This has been prophesied, practiced, and preached with increasing regularity and excitement.

> *Prophetic evangelism is not only on the radar–*
> **IT IS THE RADAR** *when it comes to the emerging harvest.*

Our book on this subject, (entitled *Prophetic Evangelism*) has exceeded all of our expectations. It has been met with great excitement and has been equal to the demand. We have also been busy offering prophetic evangelism–equipping conferences all over the nation and have witnessed great praise reports of ordinary people being used in extraordinary ways to win people to Christ by stepping out.

Now we come to the present and pregnant moment. From the jump we had a vision to release a tool to help the body of Christ implement the truths and principles of *Prophetic Evangelism*. **My sense of unfinished business centered on the response of people who made clear the need to put legs on previous concepts**. There came a cry for more practical steps and elaboration, which evolved into this all-new, fresh material. We received the vision for a combo-book that would serve both purposes. It would be fresh manifest material and a fresh training manual, all-in-one!

In Numbers 10:1-9, God told Moses to make two solid silver trumpets that would serve two crucial purposes. The first trumpet signaled a strategic summit; it was for the calling together of the army of the Lord. The second trumpet signaled the launching of a movement; it was for directing the army to break camp.

Prophetic Evangelism, our first book, is the first silver trumpet, in that we believed it signals a calling forth of the army of God to miracle evangelism and

1

supernatural soul-winning. This combo-book, *Epic Lifestyle* (the sequel and workbook for *Prophetic Evangelism*), serves as the second trumpet, with the purpose of launching you out into effective harvesting. In the Bible, when the two silver trumpets were blown together, God promised it would result in His assistance and redemption from the hand of the enemy. If you haven't gotten the first trumpet (*Prophetic Evangelism*), we recommend that you get a copy (www.propheticevangelism.org).

Now, speaking of this combo-tool epic manual that you hold in your hands, it will prove to be a much needed divine weapon in the battle for souls.

We must have a multidimensional witness, one of proclamation, presence, and power demonstration. We can't be limited to being one-weapon soul-winners. We mustn't be cramped into the confines of one dimension; God calls us to mirror His spiritual versatility of a varied, multipurpose attack on darkness through prophetic evangelism. We must take our "flow" where we've been commanded to go.

In 2 Kings 6:1-7, a group of God's people, while building an enlargement on the school for the prophets, lost an axe head when it fell off of the handle into murky waters. Elisha the prophet cut off a stick and threw it into the waters, which caused the lost tool to rise to the surface. Then the person who lost it had to reach out and pick it up for himself.

This amazing exploit occurred at a critical moment because without the axe, they could not successfully finish the work. *Epic Lifestyle* is one of those sticks that is summoning back a strategic tool for finishing the work of the Great Commission. You need a book of Acts (axe) anointing and paradigm to penetrate the dark defenses that attempt to hold treasures (souls) captive in darkness. The stick (*Epic Lifestyle*) is a divine summons to get the axe head back on your handle and to equip and encourage you to come out swinging.

God has been speaking to many about a soon-coming, historic ingathering of souls. **The Father's heart is aching with longing and determined in its search for equipped and eager laborers.** You will be released not only for marketplace discourses, but also for marketplace demonstration. So whether you teach a class with *Epic Lifestyle* or go through the workbook/new material on your own, prepare to launch out with a new edge (axe) and into a new movement.

Grace and Peace,
Sean Smith
P.S. We've used the lingo and semantics of DVD features in this workbook, so have fun with it!

How This Workbook Works

Each chapter has ten sections as follows:

1. "Favorite Scene Selections" contains Sean Smith's favorite clips from *Prophetic Evangelism.*

2. "Director's Bonus Commentary" presents the latest revelation on concepts taught in *Prophetic Evangelism,* written by Sean Smith.

3. "Deleted Footage" provides a copy that did not make the final cut in *Prophetic Evangelism* and is written by Sean Smith.

4. "Alternate Endings" presents the results desired for each chapter and is written by Sean Smith.

5. "Outtakes" countdown provides practical steps and principles to take out of each chapter and is written by Sean Smith.

6. "Scene Study" offers fill-in-the-blank questions written by Sean Smith from *Prophetic Evangelism.* For an answer key please contact pointblank-smith@aol.com.

7. "Extensive Scene Study" offers bonus fill-in-the-blank questions written by Sean Smith from *Prophetic Evangelism.* For an answer key please contact pointblanksmith@aol.com.

8. "Behind the Scenes" includes discussion questions written by Lloyd Zeigler.

9. "Cutting Room Floor" explores the application experience. It is your chance to use what you are learning in *Prophetic Evangelism* and *Epic Lifestyle* and is written by Lloyd Zeigler.

10. "The Making of an Epic" presents a journaling assignment written by Lloyd Zeigler.

Chapter 1

A Prophetic
Paradigm—Unleashed

We are entering extraordinary days. In many nations a great hunger for change is rising. The Lord is in search of history-makers and bondage-breakers who will bring about extreme change. Every day, more and more ordinary Christians are beginning to reach out to their communities, ministering through their own hurts and through their prophetic callings to meet people's needs and point them to Christ. God is looking for human vessels to be lightening rods of revelatory redemptive activity to reap the harvest in the last days. Will you join His movement?

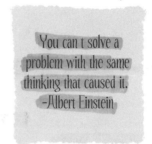

You can t solve a problem with the same thinking that caused it.
–Albert Einstein

We need a spiritual paradigm shift, which I refer to as an "out of the box" experience. Are you willing to leave your current blessing to receive a larger blessing? God will not give us purpose or direction that leaves us the same or on one plateau for very long. **Properly entering something new must be preceded by properly exiting something old.** People are limited by their own personal environment and habitat—what they hear, observe, and are taught. If you will break out from these limitations, you will undoubtedly make history in these turbulent times.

Favorite Scene Selections
Making History vs. Becoming History

Making history versus becoming history are the main options before us. *Becoming history* means we fail to make our mark; *making history* means we leave a big-time mark. Keeping pace with the competition in the struggle for the attention of the emerging generation is an uphill battle, but God will give you deer-like traction for your uphill exploits (Psalm 18:33).

We *become history* if we:

1. Turn Christianity into a philosophical exercise. We can't allow western mindsets to turn Christianity into something you just think about, versus who you are. God wants your faith expression to be full-contact and interactive.

5

2. Allow a mean-spirited, hypocritical, and nonthinking brand of Christianity to prevail. This allows us to be labeled as extreme political segments as opposed to brokers of loving mercy for a fallen planet. We can't just keep pointing out what's wrong without pointing to what is right.

3. Become museums memorializing yesteryear, sticking to out-dated traditions (nostalgia versus innovation). We can't get caught up in what we once did instead of what we need to do. We can't get "old" in our faith, where we suffer from the hardening of our spiritual arteries, blocking the desperately needed new blood of creativity and compassion.

4. Become so imbalanced in our concern with being culturally relevant that we bring a false gospel of accommodation without calling for repentance. We can't offer the promises of God without the prerequisites of God.

5. Rely on manmade methods, regardless of effectiveness, while being out of sync with the Holy Spirit. We can't limit ourselves to just hand tools; we must acquire the power tools.

6. Fail to be grasped by the successes and failures of those who have gone before us. We must reap where others have labored; we can benefit from the foundation that the Holy Spirit has laid in previous generations.

7. Allow our vision to become so hazy that we fail to know what a win looks like. We can't fail to define what a meaningful accomplishment would be. We can't be sucked into a hollow satisfaction not based on results (Amos 3:4-5).

8. Become overwhelmed and distracted by the modern working of darkness and become spectators. We shouldn't pay more attention to what the devil is doing than what God is doing.

9. Stand still and stagnate. We can't get stuck just waiting for something to happen; we must allow God to use you to make something happen. It's always amazing to see that when we live beyond our limits, stretching beyond what we ordinarily do, we see God's provision.

We *make history* if we:

1. Find the dynamic balance of being righteous, yet relevant. We must be in tune with God and then in tune with our culture.

2. Refuse to be intimidated, silenced, or unloving. We must believe that we belong; this will keep us on the cutting edge.

3. Become sensitized to open doors to share Christ with the nonbelievers whom God sends us. We can't be found too distracted or too busy to fulfill Jesus's last words, the Great Commission.

4. Cease to view God as a hobby and recommit to living and speaking the gospel regardless of the pressures to compromise. There should be no more religious games or trying to strike bargains with modern culture in order to be accepted.

5. Cooperate with the Holy Spirit to release kingdom demonstrations to go with our dynamic proclamations. We must realize that a gospel of talk is only a half-gospel.

6. Prophetically evaluate the thoughts, values, and experiences of our culture. We must begin to break down what is going down in the cultural and spiritual events around us.

> If you intend to offer Christ to the world in a way that is meaningful and relevant, you must give time and energy to a growing relationship with Him.
> — Seminary Professor Terry Wardle

7. Begin to think like missionaries and wade out into the stream of our society. We must look through the eyes of the people we're trying to reach. Status quo evangelism says, "Open the doors and they'll come." We can no longer just post the times for church programs and wait for the needy to show up.

8. Believe that we are on the stage of history to make a difference and be history-makers. We must take the gospel out of the church to the needy people around us.

9. Receive God's mantle of prophetic evangelism in this season.

Director's Bonus Commentary
Reversing the Label and Getting Uncaved

"Reversing the label" is changing your inward picture concerning the activity and assignment you are called to do. Many times when we recall a concept or think of an activity, a single word or label comes to mind. Whatever that initial predominant thought is, we are either enabled or disabled.

7

People describe witnessing as awkward, uncomfortable, pressure-filled, fearful, uneasy, and dreadful. We need to reverse the label. **The label "it's impossible" prevents us from exploits, because we won't rise up if we feel "up" isn't attainable.** We must change the connotation (our inward association) with sharing Christ. We must not only reverse the label in our thinking, but also reverse the label in the world's thinking. Many people groups embracing perversions have pushed the envelope of their beliefs into mainstream society by reversing the label. We would help our cause if we asked ourselves afresh, "What aspect of the gospel is good news to people?" To be uncaved, we must first reverse the label; this will lead to a coming-out party for the righteous!

The sorriest, bleakest, most embarrassing piece of heavenly video to be replayed in heaven will be when the prophets of God hid in caves in the times of Jezebel and Baal (1 Kings 18:4). The nation of Israel couldn't figure out whom it was going to serve, so it tried to go both ways. The prophets were not only sadly caved-in, but also deactivated; meanwhile, their nation was melting at its moral foundations.

The caved-in prophets needed to break out. When God persuaded one prophet to think and get outside the box, a nation came to its knees before a sovereign God. **Once one person catches the passionate fire of change, others will be infected as well.**

Deleted Footage
A Time for a Breakthrough

The breaker anointing is indispensible to you as a prophetic evangelist. This breakout dynamc must flow in your life, before it flows through your life. **Perhaps the greatest gap in life is the one between knowing and doing; it's the difference between intention and action.** It's the procrastination gap! In 2 Samuel 5:17-21, after being threatened and surrounded by the Philistines, David

> *The BREAKER ANOINTING is indispensable to you as a prophetic evangelist. This BREAKOUT DYNAMIC must flow in your life, before it flows through your life.*

went before the Lord to get his mind right. God told him to go against his enemies, and God would deliver the oppressors into his hands. When David broke out, God broke through the oppressors like a flashflood of water.

David renamed the geographic location Perazim, which means breakthrough. David's moment before God's presence preceded the Philistines' defeat. A breaker anointing causes you to get past what holds you back and holds you down. Let's believe that in this session, there will be similar moments for you where you will break out of limitations and break through barriers to greater fruitfulness. Perazim *must* mean more to us as prophetic evangelists than some old mountain in the Old Testament if we are to break through postmodern urban defenses and break out in our communities. You will be tested in your resolve to get breakthroughs.

"I am willing to put myself through anything; temporary pain or discomfort means nothing to me as long as I can see that the experience will take me to the next level. I am interested in the unknown, and the only path to the unknown is through breaking barriers, an often painful process."
– Diana Nyan

The point is, you must resist all resistances and oppose all opposition. Forward momentum will always be your friend. 1 John 3:8, which says, "For this purpose the Son of God was manifested, that He might destroy the works of the devil," is a mission statement for Sean Smith Ministries. I feel especially challenged by the fact that the anointing of Christ particularly manifests when you're breaking out against specific works of the devil. **Don't be afraid to go where the devil has been working—that's where God will be working through you.** Jesus will manifest in you and through you for the purpose of annihilating the darkness that comes to cloud people's minds.

Alternate Endings
Building According to the Blueprint

The first walk-away timeless truth (W.A.T.T.) to take from this chapter is that this is a crucial moment for you and your world. The decisions you make and the actions you take will definitely affect the course of history. Just like God used Peninah to provoke Hannah, secularism and pop-spirituality can have a functional purpose: creating a defining moment and forcing you to be real and to properly adjust. Now you and the church must make some changes to reach a changing world. Making changes means breaking patterns. **If you have trouble getting to a particular location in your car, you don't need a new car—you just need a new map.** Which patterns keep you from moving ahead? To break a pattern, you need a trigger event and the fuel. A trigger event is a circumstance that introduces you to the consequences of an unexamined life that makes you open to change.

9

The only way to change is first to *want* to change, and then you must do the work. Learning what does not work for you is as important as learning what does work for you. One thing to take from this lesson is the need to become aware of unproductive patterns and morph them into productive patterns.

The second W.A.T.T. to take from this lesson is that you must contend for the original blueprint. There's a group of people in the church who sense their need to witness, but because they see church as a place of social interaction and privilege, they would rather be fed than fish! Somewhere along the road, the church lost its sense of purpose; we no longer seem driven by a sense of mission. Billy Sunday once said, "More men fail through lack of purpose than through lack of talent."

The church has entrenched itself in patterns that have distanced it from the people it is called to evangelize. If you pursue your purpose, you will experience the pleasure of a breakout life. The purpose of God will lead, guide, and constrain you for the rest of your life.

The final W.A.T.T. of this chapter is that you must pursue lasting change. Don't let the devil plant the lie that this is out of the question for you. They say a new habit takes six weeks to establish. This course is 12 weeks minimally; you will have ample time to see the Holy Spirit revolutionize your life with an extreme prophetic evangelism makeover. Remember, you've already experienced the new birth; after that you should never allow any personal transformation to seem impossible. Find your place in the Son today!

Let's revisit covenants. Broken covenants affect cultures and society as a whole. Where covenants between people have been made and then broken, the land is contaminated (Isaiah 24:5). I'm convinced that part of the solution involves our relationship to a covenant-keeping God. **You must fight broken covenants with forming one of your own. By acting in the opposite spirit to your surroundings, you are positioned to bring a revolution.** Get in covenant with other prophetic evangelists and make a new covenant before the Father of lights.

Outtakes Countdown

10. Be willing to leap scared. The problem is that change involves risk, and most people are uncomfortable with risk. In spite of it all, go ahead and take the next step. Remember, taking that first risk increases your ability to take a subsequent risk.

9. "And the young shall lead them." Be flexible. There is a need to be childlike. Children aren't put off by change; they naturally gravitate towards what is new (Isaiah 43:18, 19).

8. "Let there be light." Get a fresh vision and nurture new ideas:
a. Get around big-vision believers—it will spark fresh ideas.
b. Meditate on the book of Acts paradigms—follow the Holy Spirit's blueprint.

7. When in doubt, go with your trailblazing DNA. The spiritual DNA that you possess makes it natural for you to launch into new spiritual territory; it's abnormal to become prematurely satisfied.

6. Deliberately step beyond into foreign waters. Ask yourself, "Do I really want to continue this habit and maintain the status quo, or do I want something more?" This next week, engage three new people in conversation seeking to establish a redemptive relationship with them.

5. Don't hang with homeostasis. Homeostasis is the tendency to be irresistibly drawn towards doing what you've already done. Remember that changing what you do will change others' response to you.

4. Recognize that big achievements and major exploits often come one step at a time, and one day at a time. Don't be intimidated by the need for a major personal overhaul; just stick with God's process. Refuse to allow resistances to stop you.

> Life is either a daring adventure or nothing. Avoiding danger is no safer in the long run than exposure.
> — Helen Keller

3. Take action as soon as possible. Before the feeling passes and the revelation dims—act on it! Otherwise, you will fall prey to the Law of Diminishing Intent. Time is as precious as life. The demons are deadly serious about owning opportunities; once you recognize this truth, it will motivate you as well. (Ephesians 5:16)

2. Ask God for a new breakout anointing to come upon you. Determine to live courageously. Reject boredom and leave dead religion and the religious crowd behind in exchange for a fruitful life.

1. Learn to ask yourself this question: "If I weren't so insecure and filled with anxiety, how would I act? What would I say and do?" Then, say it and do it! One of the greatest gifts God can give you is a problem to solve.

11

Prophetic Evangelism – Field Activation Manual

Scene Study
Fill in the Blanks

Q. 1. The longer you _____ something, the longer it _____ your experience.

Q. 2. In our world today, too many fear stepping out into a _____opportunity more than they fear _____ _____ on a new opportunity.

Q. 3. A confined believer loses _____, _____, and _____.

Q. 4. You must remember that the _____ you're up against today will be the floor you're going to _____ on tomorrow.

Q. 5. The hallway to spiritual outbreak is _____ _____.

Q. 6. What are the four stages of desperation?

_____
_____
_____
_____

Q. 7. What is a covenant?

_____
_____
_____

Extensive Scene Study
Bonus Questions

Q. 1. What is the purpose of a covenant?

_____
_____
_____
_____

Q. 2. Give a biblical example of radical recalibration (not mentioned in the book).

_____

_____

_____

_____

Q. 3. What event is occurring in our nation that is like a Peninah to you?

_____

_____

_____

_____

Q. 4. What were the two attempts that Elkanah made to appease Hannah, and what do they represent?

_____

_____

_____

_____

Behind the Scenes
Discussion Questions

Discussion Location: A large public pool or an open room.

Discussion Experience 1: Design a box that you feel will give your students a true confining experience. Nearly every "Fear Factor" show has some type of box. It can be as simple as a cardboard box, or very elaborate such as a Plexiglas box or a coffin. Have each of the students write down on a red sheet of paper the things that confine them from evangelizing. Have them each enter the box for the appropriate amount of time taking with them the red sheet of paper. They will leave this paper in the box as they have now put the confinement to death.

As they arise out of the box, have the rest of the students pray for them for a new life of boldness without confinement and fears holding them back. Once everyone has had their "out of the box" experience, have them write down on a blue piece of paper how they are committed to live now that this confinement has no power over them.

1. Discuss a difficult season in your life that you have experienced.
   a. What was its divine seed? Meaning, what heavenly purpose did it serve?
   b. What attributes have you developed as a result?
   c. What lesson(s) have you learned?

2. God has called you to move.
   a. What do you have to leave behind today to move?
   b. Are you confined in any way?
   c. Describe your confinement and prescribe the remedy.

3. "Once you bust out of where you've been confined, it is impossible to get you to conform back to your original dimension."
   -Sean Smith, Prophetic Evangelism
   a. Revisit a confinement in your life that you have overcome. Describe that confinement.
   b. Now that you are free, it will be nearly impossible to conform back (John 8:36).

4. "Fight the enemy by speaking the word."
   -Sean Smith, Prophetic Evangelism

   Write a list of words and/or phrases that describe the things you struggle with. Search for scriptures to counteract these specific attacks. List the struggle and the verse side by side, and begin to memorize and meditate on them daily.

Discussion Experience 2: Have the students take turns jumping off of the high dive, as the author spoke about being at the edge of the board and jumping in.
1. Name some famous heroes.
   a. Name some famous lunatics. Understand that the lunatics and the heroes of this world possess an equal potential for good. Lunatics lack relation to a cause.
   b. What are some causes of these famous heroes?
   c. What is your cause?

2. A cause inspires a mission. What is your cause statement?

3. What would a positive change in your life cost you? What would staying the same cost you?

Cutting Room Floor
Application

"As long as your complacency level is high, you won't produce or achieve your objectives."

"Too many people fear stepping out into a new opportunity more than they fear missing out on a new opportunity."

– *Sean Smith*, Prophetic Evangelism

Individual Application: Find a person in desperation such as a homeless person or someone with a severe addiction or need, and ask the Holy Spirit for the words to pray for that person. Pray for the person verbally before you leave him or her.

Group Application: Put together a neighborhood outreach. Let the Holy Spirit show you where it is to be located. Go door to door informing the people of the "festival." Go home and pray; let the Holy Spirit show you who is suppose to lead each part of that outreach so that it is tailored to that specific neighborhood. During the outreach, let God show you how to make the outreach unique and individual to this specific neighborhood. **No rules, just right approach.**

The Making of an Epic
Journaling

1. Write your testimony.

2. If you were asked to describe your relationship with God, what would you say?

3. Answer the following questions:
   a. Why do you believe in God?
   b. How has God changed your life?
   c. Is your testimony living in the past, or is God continually real, personal, and powerful in your life from day to day?

4. If you were to write a covenant with God, what would your covenant say?

5. What did you learn from the application in this chapter?
   a. How did it make you feel?
   b. What were your fears?
   c. How did you pray?
   d. What did God show you?
   e. What were your obstacles?

Journal Notes

Journal Notes

Chapter 2

The Spirit of Burning

The world needs full contact with all-out displays of New Testament spirituality grounded in Jesus. These times demand radical followers of Christ, willing to obey God's will at all cost.

> We have to get people beyond dedication and into fascination.
> — Mike Bickle

> Those who hear not the music, think the dancer s mad.
> — Classic proverb

Favorite Scene Selection
Rejection: This Present Darkness Weapon of Choice

While our spiritual forefathers were threatened with the guillotine and burning stakes, we are often faced with social ostracism and personal disapproval. **While ancient Christians steamrolled through the swords of torture aimed against them, some modern Christians roll away from the "butter knives" of ridicule aimed against them.** It is easy to see why the guillotine was menacing, but how has rejection in our age become such an abnormal scourge? Part of the answer is found in the lost discipline called the fear of the Lord. This fear is not cowering but reverencing our awesome God.

Whomever or whatever you fear the most will dictate and direct your life. You can unleash the soul winner within by walking in a greater awareness of God's Word than public opinion. Meditating on scriptures and the attributes of God will definitely aid in this quest.

Another part of the answer is found in how much we feed on the praises or acceptance of man rather than being grounded in the love of the Father. **To whatever extent you are unduly uplifted by the compliments of the crowd, you will be unduly diminished by their criticisms.** Criticism is a compliment when you're doing the right thing; Christ yearned for people's conversions, not their compliments.

Finally, I believe the most underrated solution for this weapon of choice is holy companionship. In Acts 4:23, after Peter and John had been persecuted by the Sanhedrin, they went to their own companions. What resulted was not a licking of their wounds, but the unleashing of boldness, signs, and wonders. As you gather with other on-fire, crazy-loving soul winners, you will be nurtured in prophetic evangelism, and your boldness will return. I'm convinced this is a major reason why Jesus sent the disciples out two-by-two, so that each could help wipe the dust of rejection off of the other. Link up with a prophetic evangelist accountability support partner, and you will take a weapon out of the enemy's hand.

Psalm 2:2-4
The kings of the earth set themselves,
And the rulers take counsel together,
Against the LORD and against His Anointed, saying,
"Let us break Their bonds in pieces
And cast away Their cords from us."
He who sits in the heavens shall laugh;
The LORD shall hold them in derision.

Kings and rulers had the power to exert great influence upon their day and lead people in the direction of their choice. Today, we have talking heads, TV hosts, reality TV, and music icons selling their philosophies of life and spiritual matters to millions. Opinion-makers are feverishly busy dictating tastes, biases, and preferences. Yet this passage tells us that their attempt to "front" or intimidate God's purposes will be so harmless at the end of the day that it only makes God chuckle. You can believe that! The Bible says, "Let the redeemed of the Lord say so" (Psalm 107:1). In modern translation that means you must have your say, despite the volume of the modern airwaves, or what the "spin doctors" are saying!

Many times a lie is sold to us that you must be able to answer all objections before you dare to lock horns in evangelism. But check this out! **New believers who can't necessarily defend what they believe lead the largest number of unbelievers to Christ.** They are so thrilled and exhilarated to be saved, to have found the answer, that they are passionate about getting the word out. They enthusiastically tell their friends, most of who are unbelievers. It doesn't matter if you have been saved one year or twenty years, you can still discover this passion and bust out of your box! Don't buy the lie for a second that you have to be a preacher to lead people to Christ. Just get out of the box of familiarity and revisit the joy of your salvation.

Director's Bonus Commentary
Getting Epic and Freeing the Voice

Having an epic life happens after making an epic stand. Getting epic has every-thing to do with getting to the place where nothing else matters. **We must seek opportunities over security.** Security is all relative anyway. Being in your des-tiny in the will of God is as secure as it gets. Everything else is about as safe as a fly buzzing around a bug zapper.

It is only when you decide to pursue an epic life that there can be full acti-vation of your gifts and anointing. Early in my walk, I felt inspired by God to give His kingdom my best and to believe God for the impossible. Pastor Bill Johnson was right when he said, "It is unnatural for a Christian to not have an appetite for the impossible."

Getting epic will cause you to move from religious infatuations to heavenly romance. Once you kiss the Son, you'll embrace His pearl—His inheritance in the earth. This resolve happens because you let go of the emergency brakes in your walk and allow full-throttle Christianity to break the sound barrier. Don't be afraid to be different—this will prove to be your strength. Getting epic means experiencing the divine fusion of an extreme awakening to your ultimate destiny and capturing God's fiery spirit. Getting epic must begin with you getting alone with the epic God who has overcome the world (Mark 3:14 15). In modern trans-lation, "It's your season to step into this blessing." What are you waiting on? History is waiting for you to give it a shove; you go girl! You go boy!

Freeing the Voice

To free the voice is to free the person. History is replete with God's power made known through ordinary people finding their voice. In Mark 16:8, Mary Magdalene and Mary the mother of Jesus were terrified by the words of the angel, which seemed to leave them speechless. They left the heavenly visitor quickly, "but said nothing to anyone for they were afraid." What caused them to freeze up? After Jesus visited them they were ripe to be hyped; they were launched into a, "I dare you to shut me up" witnessing roll. **Yet these first prophetic evangelists of the resurrection found their voice in the midst of their drama.** The first prophetic evangelists had to overcome fear and make their voices heard. Things haven't changed in two millenniums; we still come to victory by winning this battle.

Scriptures declare that they told others, obviously shaking the influence of the dreaded deaf and dumb spirit. A deaf and dumb spirit wants to shut you up and shut you down. Like the incident where the disciples were unsuccessful in casting out this demonic spirit (Mark 9), you will be challenged to shake off its influence and free your voice. In this incident, Jesus got this young boy's voice free, yet it was only after shaking things up a bit. In Mark 9:27, Jesus took this formerly deaf and dumb spirit, this harassed young person, by the hand and lifted him up causing him to arise. Jesus is here to do the same for you in this moment; just ask Him.

The first prophetic evangelists had to overcome fear and make their voices heard. Things HAVEN'T CHANGED IN TWO MILLENNIUMS; *we still come to victory by winning this battle.*

Deleted Footage
Speculation vs. Revelation

Internal perspective relieves external pressure. When you know what others don't, you will be released to go places where others fear to tread. A revelation delivers you from calculating decisions based on your immediate consequences. You are God's voice to your city. **God drops off a revelation to a church and to an individual in order to rescue a community.** Revelation is about your capacity to carry a truth and to be built into the new thing the Lord is creating. "Lite" Christianity is when the adversary of your soul comes to downsize your revelation to speculation. Speculation is defined as the thinking of a man deliberating with himself, which becomes a barrier. Speculation is a belief based on

A revelation delivers you from CALCULATING DECISIONS *based on your immediate consequences.*

flimsy feelings that gets bum-rushed by reality. Speculation has the silicon implants that look like muscle but have no endurance or substance. Revelatory people are full-throttle warriors; speculators are full-time worriers.

A revelation releases moral strength and deep conviction. A speculation gets defeated in the locker room before the outreach. In Acts 4, Peter and John faced opposition. These men were under persecution, but they didn't flinch. Persecution and threats expose speculation and unfold revelation. All their oppressors could say was that "they had been with Jesus." The Sanhedrin did not have a full burst of fury against the young apostles but wanted to experiment to see how far they would go, and they definitely went the distance.

Speculation is a "wanna-be" and revelation is the real deal. Speculation is a pea-shooter, where revelation is an atomic bomb. In Acts 5:33-39, a Pharisee named Gamaliel stood up to warn the persecutors of the early church. He told them if the apostles were in speculation, then their movement would fold like all the other papier-mâché human movements, but if they were people of revelation—there would be no stopping their runaway-freight train-God movement. Revelation feeds crazy love and vice versa. God wants to download a revelation to you!

Alternate Endings
A Fiery Spirit and A Furious Love Affair

The first walk-away timeless truth (W.A.T.T.) from this chapter revolves around super extreme desire. Desire means "appetite, longing for, a craving." It's an inner motivation, a propelling and compelling energizing fuel. Michelangelo is quoted as saying, "Lord, grant that I may always desire more than I can accomplish!" Crazy love desire motivates you to learn, accomplish, and become all that God wants for you.

God wants to sow a fiery seed of tremendous impact in your heart today. See yourself as a minister who has been made into a flame of fire (Hebrews 1:7). Jesus has been kindling (Luke 12:49) your heart or you would not be taking this course.

MICHELANGELO *is quoted as saying,"Lord, grant that I may always desire more* THAN I CAN ACCOMPLISH!*"*

Once you achieve God's super desire, there will be no turning back. Remember you're not too young, not too old, not too sophisticated, or too simple to have a fiery desire to be used. Your greatest joy may be a conversation away; it may be across the street, a classroom, or an office away from you.

The second W.A.T.T. is to see the crazy lover within awakened. Know that within every born-again soul, God deposits a "crazy love" or a "zeal for the Father's house" to consume them. We know that perfect love casts out fear (1 John 4:18), so when the crazy lover within is awakened, you will throw off the fear of man. Begin to pray for a baptism of holy affections to ignite you.

This chapter is also intended to teach you how to sustain the fire. **A fiery spirit is a prerequisite for prophetic evangelism.** A lot of people get excited about soul winning for a period, but then their zeal cools off. God wants you to keep the fire burning. God is not after an on-fire activity, but an on-fire life. British author

G. K. Chesterton called the Christian life a "furious love affair." To sustain the fire, the ingredients have to be right for your fire to burn. **The spiritual fire of God within you will only burn as brightly as the conditions of your life. Your life mustn't be about ashes, but about embers; not about past fires, but a current flame.** Remember the burning bush catches more attention and gets more looks than the barren bush.

Certain actions will set your life on fire. Two in particular are to live the Word of God while witnessing the activity of God's power. Get around people and places in which God is moving mightily. Ultimately just walk with Jesus in an intimate way and the fire within will rise. Worshippers make the best warriors because they always have fire on their censer. Have you made this choice a permanent resolve? After this session, you get your Ph.D. (passion, hunger, and desire) in prophetic evangelism! Congrats!

> The world has never been moved by the mild or moderate. The choice that we are presented with in the closing days of history may not be between the mad and the sane, but between the holy and the holy madness.
> — Winkie Pratney

Outtakes Countdown

10. Identify the passion-killers in your spiritual journey with God. Clean up what motivates you and go for it! Blow the dust off and bring to the surface those things that inspire passion in your life.

9. Meditate on the themes of God's extreme love for you (Romans 8:38-39, Song of Solomon 4:9, John 3:16, Luke 7:47). God will cause fresh passion to rise up inside of you as the Word and the Holy Spirit reveal the Father's heart to you.

8. Surround yourself with extreme crazy lovers. Get around the most fiery spiritual people you can. Read biographies of men and women who are or were on fire for Christ. Attend conferences and find resources that will impart the flame. Position your heart before the fireplace of God's presence.

7. Be willing to "fake it 'till you make it." Allow the actions and responses of passion to flow through you, and the feelings will follow your decision.

6. Begin to use affectionate and passionate terms to describe God and your love for Him. Remember that your tongue is the rudder of your boat. The spirit placed within you cries out "Daddy," touching an affectionate spot that the Almighty holds for His kids (Romans 8:15, Galatians 4:6).

5. Deliberately let yourself go in worship and praise (2 Samuel 6:14-22). Keep dancing until the formalities fall off of you. Act as if no one is watching but God; this will translate into effectiveness in witnessing.

4. Get a devotional tune-up. Begin to tune into the fascination of the angels. Use prayer time, private worship, and Word time to "beef up" your inner history with God.

3. Go further out on a limb for God's fruit. Go public today with crazy love for the King and His kingdom. You won't go public if you feel that your faith is a private affair. Unleash your inner soul winner and that suppressed deliverer within you today!

2. Refuse to burn on any spiritual fuel other than God's premium crazy love. By doing this, you will protect yourself from burning out.

1. Remember who is really on trial. A certain young man after visiting the National Gallery of Art told the guard that he didn't like the paintings. The guard replied, "Son, these paintings aren't on trial; you are!"

Prophetic Evangelism - Field Activation Manual
Scene Study
Fill in the Blanks

Q. 1. Crazy love has the components of both compelling _____ and the
_____ to abandon all.

Q. 2. Modern culture is not drawn to Christianity because the little they are
exposed to is not extreme enough for them.
True   False

Q. 3. What are the two downfalls of people-pleasing?

_____

_____

_____

_____

Q. 4. Sometimes you've got to go through the _____ to get to your

_____.

Q. 5. What is the recipe for crazy love?

_____

_____

_____

_____

Q. 6. There are many things that we don't have control over, but we can control
the _____ and _____ with which we live our lives.

Extensive Scene Study
Bonus Questions

Q. 1. What is the statement below mean, according to *Prophetic Evangelism*?
"Don't let the residue of rejection cling to you."

_____

_____

_____

_____

Q. 2. What does Jerusalem represent in the story of David and the Jebusites?

_____

_____

_____

_____

Q. 3. Who made the simple washing of hands infamous?

_____

_____

Q. 4. One will never _____ effectively until they can _____ freely.

Behind the Scenes
Discussion Questions

Discussion Location: Classroom

1. In the book, *Prophetic Evangelism*, passion is defined as a compelling emotion or a strong desire for something. What are three things you are passionate about today?

2. The people of today's culture reject Christianity because most of what they see is not extreme enough for them.
    a. List some extreme things modern culture is drawn to today such as reality television, magicians, etc.
    b. How could we show them the extremes of Christianity?

3. What are your top ambitions worthy of giving up your life? Where does proclaiming the gospel of Jesus fall on that list?

4. When have you chosen to please God instead of people?
    a. How did it make you feel?
    b. What would you have missed out on if you had chosen to please people instead of God?

5. Describe a past experience in which you were rejected or ridiculed for sharing your faith.

Compare the negative feelings that you may be feeling to the worth of the human soul. Learn to wipe the dust off your feet by letting your friends encourage you.

6. Paul's life was an infectious one.
   a. Like Paul, talk about how you've had an effect on someone's life.
   b. How has another contagious Christian had an effect on you?
   c. Talk about some people whom you would like your life to impact.

7. We all agree that we've got to have a place in our lives where we establish a daily time for the presence of God.
   a. Do you have that time?
   b. When is that time?
   c. What happens during that time?

Cutting Room Floor
Application

Honor Chair: Honor Chair should be done in an intimate setting, a closed room or structure. It works by placing one chair in the center of the room. Choose one person to sit in that chair as one person at a time kneels before him and begins to speak truth, hope, and encouragement into his life. This tool allows others to say what is on their hearts. Let God direct your mouth to begin the healing process. The person in the chair may not speak; he can only receive the words into his heart.

This can be done one person at a time, for as long as the Spirit allows. This is used to shake the dust off of past bad experiences and rejection. At the end of this experience, allow for some time for God to speak His love to the person. Once we are filled with love from others and the love of God, we are now ready to pour out love to the lost.

The Making of an Epic
Journaling

1. Page 33 in *Prophetic Evangelism* says that sometimes you've got to go through a gutter to get to your goal. Write about a "gutter" experience or a time you've had to endure to get to this point in your life. How has it made you better?

2. Rejection is a cruel taskmaster; the Bible taught how to shake the dust of rejection from your feet. Name one time when rejection discouraged you and how God enabled you to overcome it.

3. What areas of your life do you need God's fire the most and how do you think that fire would change your life (be specific).

Journal Notes

Journal Notes

Chapter 3

The Fusion of the Revelatory and the Redemtive

You can't let people get away with just getting an earful. Vintage Christianity is about giving them an eyeful.

"A man has no ears to that which experience has given him no access."
– *Friedrich Nietzsche*

Favorite Scene Selections
Divine Synchronization

"Divine Synchronization" is my favorite section of this chapter because it is the basis for the entire book. In Luke 5:4-9, scripture sets forth the divine blueprint for prophetic evangelism and builds the best case for its immediate implementation. Peter's human methodologies left him without a catch; Jesus's divine prescription brought in a multiboat-sinking catch of a lifetime. Afterward, Jesus told them that they would catch men. This set forth a supernatural download and the release of the anointing for "at Your word" mass harvesting.

As you position yourself to share your faith, Jesus will give you direction to make your sharing effective. Prophetic action is based on prophetic "at Your words" that release catches. **"At Your word" moments are when God speaks to you and opens up doors for incredible new territories.** When Peter said "nevertheless" in Luke 5:5 and broke with past patterns, he came to the fruitful point of divine synchronization. Another term for synchronization is "vibe-ing." God wants you to capture His vibe. If you're in His tribe, you can catch His vibe (John 10:27). As Bobby Conner says, "There must come a swift synchronization between God's will and our walk." If you obey the "at Your words" in your life, you will be a boat-sinking fisherman, coming home with the big catch.

If you obey the "AT YOUR WORDS" in your life, you will be a boat-sinking fisherman, coming home with the big catch.

Luke 5:10

...and so also were James and John, the sons of Zebedee, who were partners with Simon. And Jesus said to Simon, "Do not be afraid. From now on you will catch men."

In giving Peter a prophetic instruction, Jesus was ordaining a system of attack on unbelief and darkness in men's souls. This system would involve prophetic promptings that would direct future disciples in winning souls. Jesus also addressed the predominate emotion—fear—which comes when you step away from something you *can* do without God to something you *can't* do without Him. It is natural to feel some apprehension, but go ahead and take the jump of dependence on God anyway.

Luke 5:5-6

But Simon answered and said to Him, "Master, we have toiled all night and caught nothing; nevertheless at Your word I will let down the net." And when they had done this, they caught a great number of fish, and their net was breaking.

I realize that I must overcome the urge to fall into past patterns and personal ruts of cultural habits. You can't allow your culture to squeeze you into its mold.

a. **"Nevertheless"** means in spite of what my five senses tell me or my personal experiences or previous training, I will follow your instructions.

b. **"From now on you will catch men."** In other words, the principle you have learned in this incident will operate in winning the lost. Prophetic action based on the prophetic word releases Holy Spirit exploits. Jesus is still calling you to launch out into the deep.

Another picture of divine synchronization, "vibe-ing," is found in Mark 6:47-51. Jesus told the disciples to go across a lake to the other side. Then after the storm and wind broke out against them, they found themselves straining to row, not making any headway. How many of us have been found struggling in our divine assignments? We must recognize Jesus and get Him in our boat, which is the key that will conquer the resistance. Their scenario was a test in recognizing Christ's movement in the heat of battle. Once they passed this initial challenge, divine synchronization was engaged when Jesus got in their boat; immediately the storm and resistance ceased, and they reached their destination.

As you follow God's movement and direction, resistances will submit to the revelations that He will show you, while you're involved in outreach activities. Today, as you go to witness, Jesus wants to get in your boat, and when He does, you go from mere evangelism to prophetic evangelism.

Divine synchronization is the key for heaven invading earth. **God desires our witnessing to be interactive, which requires us to enter into a quality of a prophetically charged, attuned friendship with the Holy Spirit.** True spirituality is always a spiritual response to the Father. It is God who reaches out to us, speaks to us, and enables us to hear His voice—God is always the initiator. The bottom line is that genuine results come only from divine initiative and your response ability.

> TRUE SPIRITUALITY *is always a spiritual response to the* FATHER.

Director's Bonus Commentary
The Arrow Is Beyond You

In 1 Samuel 20:20-22, Jonathan says to David, "If the arrows are beyond you, go out from here for the Lord is sending you out." In the original language, the word "beyond" means "further out there" and "beyond your place of current position." Similar to David's word, God is declaring, "the arrow is beyond you." This represents two significant principles for you. Firstly, this speaks of God launching you into new territory that he has pre-arranged for you to take. Let's believe God to take schools, cities, blocks, campuses, work places, and neighborhoods. God is into real estate! David went out into new territory.

Secondly, this speaks of the weaponry you need being beyond your current position. You need the arrows from heaven because earth-bound arrows won't get it done since gravity pulls those arrows down. Witnessing in this day requires the supernatural, which is out there beyond mere human persuasion or manipulation. **You must realize that what it takes to reach this generation requires you to launch into new spiritual territory and implement the prophetic in your weaponry; otherwise, you will miss the mark.** You need divine insight to ignite your witness. An unexpressed thought is dead! You need the tools of the Spirit to free the captive spirit of humanity. Truth is supernaturally generated; it is not manufactured within the framework of the natural.

The prophetic anointing is a revelatory release that sees beyond the present situation and brings the purpose of God into sharp focus. It is a revelation of

The PROPHETIC ANOINTING *is a revelatory release that sees beyond the present situation and brings the* PURPOSE OF GOD *into sharp focus.*

the mind of God. Revelation sparks passion; it brings a sense of His purpose and destiny for your life. Revelation provides spiritual eyes that see, releasing understanding to the heart. Without the prophetic, an unbeliever will be only superficially exposed to a superficial Christianity. In the spiritual realm, thought is the flashpoint of creative power, so if God thinks it, it is happening. **When God gives us His thoughts, it's already a done deal in the spirit realm, and when we obey, it's manifested in the physical realm.** That's why it is so important to receive one of God's thoughts, and equally important to act on it!

The prophetic anointing causes an individual to go through a dealing or event before the masses go through it. It causes you to be on the front end of methodology and yields a fresh sound. You, as a prophetic evangelist, are truly dancing to the beat of a different drummer. Your decision to take the truth of prophetic evangelism to heart is proof that God has put a prophetic designation on your life. It is the law of attraction: what you are attracted to is in symphony with what lies within you!

If we trained prophetic people to be evangelistic and evangelistic people to be prophetic, we would be dangerous and discerning, walking through divine doors with *dunamis* power. The gospel ought to be a surprise attack. Being prophetic is being led of the Spirit in such a way that it throws darkness off guard.

> Every believer has the potential of utilizing the prophetic anointing in outreach to the non-Christian community.
> —*Ernest Gentile*

The difference between programmatic evangelism and prophetic evangelism is likened to the difference between the impact of a bird hunter's rifle with buckshot and a sniper's rifle with scope and bullets. The bullet is meant to devastate a small target, and buckshot relies more on accidental chance hits due to its volume.

God's power and witness is FUNDAMENTALLY *necessary for you to accomplish* HEAVEN'S BLUEPRINT *for your generation.*

The substance and nature of prophecy exceed the limit that the human mind is capable of thinking or imagining. What is attacking and attaching itself to this generation demands that you access the mind of Christ and flow in prophetic evangelism. God's power and witness is fundamentally necessary for you to accomplish heaven's blueprint for your generation.

Deleted Footage
Developing Prophetic Evangelism Tendencies

Let's revisit Revelation 19:10 and establish some foundations for prophetic evangelism. Revelation 19:10 tells us that the testimony of Christ is the Spirit of prophecy. 1 Corinthians 1:6-7 tells us, "even as the testimony of Christ (spirit of prophecy) was confirmed in you, so that you come short in no gift." **Every Spirit-filled believer possesses and has access to the Spirit of prophecy.**

The original Greek word for testimony used in Revelation 19:10 means evidence or witness. Part of the evidence that we have Jesus Christ in us, is that we can prophesy or have a prophetic witness, which is prophetic evangelism. Still not convinced? In Exodus God told Moses to prophesy to Pharaoh to let God's people go. Moses doubted his abilities to flow like that and tried to excuse himself with his speech impediment. Then God said that Aaron would speak to Pharaoh and Moses would speak to Aaron and put words in his mouth. Aaron would be Moses' spokesman (Exodus 4:10-15). Aaron was flowing in prophecy by his prophetic attachment to Moses.

You have a prophetic attachment to the Ultimate Prophet, Jesus Christ, and through this connection you are able to receive words. Just as Aaron received words from Moses, you too are able. You are the Ultimate Prophet's spokesperson to see the liberation of souls.

In this "Deleted Footage" section, I want to give you some keys I've found in honing in on prophetic evangelism. Luke 15 presents God-given parables that obviously illustrate evangelism.

Luke 15:8-10
"Or what woman, having ten silver coins, if she loses one coin, does not light a lamp, sweep the house, and search carefully until she finds it? 9 And when she has found it, she calls her friends and neighbors together, saying, 'Rejoice with me, for I have found the piece which I lost!' 10 Likewise, I say to you, there is joy in the presence of the angels of God over one sinner who repents."

The parable of the lost coin reveals the following principles:

Principle 1: Soul Appreciation ("if she loses one coin").

This principle speaks of the need to value the lost and realize their worth to the Redeemer. As you appreciate something, you develop an eye for it. Artists love art, musicians love music, and by doing so they develop an eye for art or an ear for music. This allows them to pick up on the nuances and subtle characteristics that aid in their respective fields. **This soul appreciation elevates your spiritual senses in opportunities for prophetic evangelism.** You begin to see and hear things that you weren't previously picking up on.

If you had ten pieces of silver and you lost one, that would adversely affect you and thus give you a sense of urgency. You and I must have urgency for reaching people with the gospel message.

Principle 2: Opportunity Illumination ("does not light a lamp").

This principle speaks of an important key of taking the prophetic to the marketplace (Luke 11:33). When this woman lit a lamp, she took it where the lost coin was, where the darkness kept it lost. We must realize that God will release the prophetic outside the church walls to evangelize the lost. "Lighting a lamp" also refers to receiving God's illumination and insight in our spirit as we step into divine appointments (Proverbs 20:27).

Principle 3: Spirit Activation ("sweep the house").

This principle speaks of stirring up your spirit and getting your spirit at attention. When you sweep, you're removing the dust that accumulates for the lack of activity in that area. **We often miss God's signals because we've become dull in that area.** We must stay sensitive to the Holy Spirit's promptings. What you key into, you can see into!

Oswald Chambers rightly said, "The need to perceive is the most vital need of the Christian worker today." As workers we have to get used to the revelation that redemption is the only reality."

"Sweep the house" also speaks of establishing an atmosphere for evangelism and the prophetic. As we worship and draw near to God, we will accomplish this profound objective.

Oswald Chambers rightly said,
"The NEED TO PERCEIVE *is the most vital* NEED
of the Christian worker today."

Principle 4: Prophetic Observation ("search carefully until").

This principle speaks of developing the discipline of constant awareness; we must live focused lives. Effectiveness in prophetic evangelism rises as you pay attention to the Holy Spirit's movement as well as what comes up in your spirit. We must be released to continue to step out until we become fluent in "finding lost coins" (winning people to Christ).

In Matthew 10:16, Jesus tells us "to be wise as serpents, yet innocent as doves." One thing you must know about serpents is that a serpent is consciously focused and sensitive to its environment. A serpent has an extra-sensory organ in the roof of its mouth. In fact, a serpent flicks out its tongue to collect particles from its surroundings and deposits it in this extra-sensory organ called "Jacobson's organ," which processes the particles taken in. It allows for a sharpened sense of smell, phenomenal eyesight, and the ability to detect motion and vibrations.

Effectiveness in prophetic evangelism rises as you pay attention to the Holy Spirit's movement as well as what comes up in your spirit.

Jesus is challenging you and me to constantly take readings of our surrounding to detect God's motion and the vibration of a lost person's empty heart. You don't have "Jacobson's organ," but you do have Jacob's ladder (Genesis 28:12), which is a clear path to exercise and experience heaven's resources.

"With every opportunity to trust God, we also have the opportunity to fall, through unmet expectations or disappointment. We have no guarantee of success, but each time we do trust, we add to our skill and we get better at it."
– *Tom Clegg*

Judge *Eido*

"Too often a player decides what move he will make before he receives the ball. This is often a mistake. Reading and reacting to the defender must be stressed."
– *Coach Pete Newell*

Mark 6:49-51
And when they saw Him walking on the sea, they supposed it was a ghost, and cried out; 50 for they all saw Him and were troubled. But immediately He talked with them and said to them, "Be of good cheer! It is I; do not be afraid."

Revisiting Mark 6:47-51, Jesus calmed the storm while walking past a boat full of disciples who were initially oblivious to Christ. The Greek word for "saw" Him in this instance (verse 49) is *"eido."* *Eido* means "to be aware, to discern, to inspect, to experience any state or condition, to be sure of and to perceive." If you don't sensitize yourself, opportunities pass you by before you have a chance to respond to them.

We must identify and eliminate numbing influences. To adequately function in the prophetic, you must be filled with the Word (Jeremiah 5:13). 1 Corinthians 2:12 says that "we have received the Spirit which is of God; that we might know (*eido*) the things that are freely given to us of God." The Holy Spirit allows us to *eido* the things that God is releasing to us. You were made to recognize God!

In evangelism opportunities, God points out keys to our situation. **If you can pick up on what God is pointing out, the thing perceived becomes the thing received.** God's promptings register in many diverse ways. Too often people evangelize with a mindset that negates the supernatural. We don't go there (cooperate with the supernatural), and it goes hand in hand with the fact that we are unaware of the Holy Spirit's prophetic promptings.

How do these Holy Spirit promptings register?
a. You have a chance encounter with just the right person.
b. You experience a persistent, growing thought or conviction.
c. Something from the Bible leaps onto the stage of your consciousness.
d. Something said in conversation sticks out or lights up.
e. An opportunity suddenly opens up, revealing God's fingerprints.
f. It becomes harder to stop the more you try to hold back.

Here are six steps by Winkie Pratney from his book, *Ultimate Core*, on how to develop prophetic perception:
1. Stay sensitive to the promptings of the Holy Spirit (2 Peter 1:21).
2. Cultivate the sense of the presence of God (1 Corinthians 14:24-25).
3. Love people and love the nation (Romans 9:3).
4. Change themes as fast as God gives them to you. In different times different abuses attracted the prophet's attention. They never got stuck with one pet slogan (Isaiah 1:10).
5. Don't back off on the truth (Ezekiel 2:6-7).
6. Look beyond the limits of your time. The prophetic heart a) sees the past in the present, b) the future in the past, and c) the future in the present. The walls of time go down and the vision of the prophet leaps the boundaries of our immediacy. You receive tremendous power for life and ministry when you trade deciding for discerning.

Effective discernment requires that we be open to surprises to the wonderful and mysterious encounters God may have for us. John Wimber defined divine appointments as an appointed time in which God reveals Himself to an individual or group through spiritual gifts or other supernatural phenomena. As a prophetic evangelist, you will become so much more effective if you understand intuition, perception, and impressions.

Three definitions will help you:
1. Intuition—knowledge that is arrived at spontaneously, independent of reason or inquiry.
2. Perception—denotes the act of apprehending by means of the senses or intuitive awareness.
3. Impressions—often interpreted as having a gut feeling or being aware of having that certain feeling about something.

> *You receive tremendous power for* LIFE *and* MINISTRY *when you trade deciding for discerning.*

Look for God to divinely arrange these encounters to demonstrate His kingdom.

Alternate Endings
A #1 Combo with a Super-sized Flow

The first walk-away timeless truth (W.A.T.T.) in this chapter must begin with getting a full revelation of the dynamic combo of the prophetic and evangelistic gifts. Combination moves are what win in wrestling. An experienced wrestler typically counters with an isolated move. The devil has been wrestling for a while. You must leave this session convinced of the importance of prophetic evangelism and your call to function in it.

Prophetic evangelism will look different through you than through the next Christian, yet God ordains fruit in every life. This revelation will cause you to be sold out to this spiritual tool. Recently a prophetic minister stood up at a conference in the Pacific Northwest and stated, "God impressed upon my heart that P.E. (prophetic evangelism) is on God's heart in this season." Could the supernatural and the prophetic be the missing ingredients in modern evangelism in the west?

This revelation of prophetic evangelism will continue to grow on you and will bring you a fresh desire to step into witnessing opportunities. This tremendous fruit of prophetic evangelism will demand that you be bold in its use. The Bible instructs every believer to seek, earnestly desire, and covet to move in the gift of prophecy. **No gift or flow of the Holy Spirit ever comes to the casual believer who has a take-it-or-leave-it attitude.** Decide today that you can't live without the Holy Spirit's touch. What you can't live without, you won't do without.

The second W.A.T.T. involves recognizing your "flow," how God uses you in prophetic evangelism, and what situations summon your gift. You must expect and anticipate the Holy Spirit and His giftings to manifest through you. Give God space in your day to move in prophetic evangelism

This REVELATION *of prophetic evangelism will* CONTINUE TO GROW ON YOU *and will bring you a fresh* DESIRE *to step into witnessing opportunities.*

through you. David didn't take out Goliath in King Saul's armor, but with David's own flow of using his "nuclear," personally proven slingshot.

Begin to step out and catalogue how God uses you; this will greatly help you recognize when the "flow" comes again. Remember, sometimes you have to step into the moment to maximize your flow. Some people sit back spectating, waiting for a word instead of initiating based on God's Word already given to them.

Stirring up your gifting (2 Timothy 1:6) will prove to be crucial for you and those to whom you are called. In the original, the word "stir" means to kindle up, zeal, and to inflame one's mind. By completing the *Epic Lifestyle,* you will increase your knowledge about this gifting, which will stir up prophetic evangelism within you. We've already talked about strongly desiring this to operate in your life so you can be a blessing to many.

You stir up your giftings by staying full of the Holy Spirit through consecrating and dedicating your whole life to walking in the Spirit. Remember, gifts are not to promote your reputation, but God's. One of the biggest keys is to make yourself available to God as an instrument in His hands. Be willing to go with the gospel and wade into the pools of human need. Ultimately, your highest purpose is to display the essence of Christ to your generation.

Outtakes Countdown

10. Ask the Holy Spirit to direct you to the right people and to give you His words and feelings for those people. Pay attention to any mental pictures and things that spontaneously stand out while witnessing.

9. Remember to seek to touch God's heart before you seek to touch the hearts

of the unchurched. Begin with the vertical and the horizontal will be facilitated. God's touch will prove to be the deciding factor in touching their hearts.

8. Follow the formula of Proverbs 3:5-6. The Holy Spirit's guidance is mapped out in the following steps:
Trust in God completely.
Keep your heart fully in it.
Forgo your own reading of things.
Acknowledge God in the midst of every situation.
Expect the direction to come—accurately and with clarity.

7. What you don't value, you won't vibe with. You have to prioritize evangelism and the gift of prophecy to vibe with prophetic evangelism. Additionally, you won't be where you don't feel that you belong.

6. Practice prophetic evangelism by praying for unsaved friends. Ask the Holy Spirit what's on His agenda for them and pray it through. You can follow up your sensings by verifying with your friends through normal conversation.

5. No longer alienate yourself from other streams. Recognize that God spreads the wealth of His kingdom amongst the whole body of Christ. Embrace all God's weapons and arsenals in the battle for souls. Attend conferences that don't speak to your strengths or offer your favorite speakers.

4. Link up with other giftings in outreaches. Having different giftings allows for a fuller expression of Christ and provides more tools in winning souls.

3. Know that prophecy springs from the same anointing and inspiration that causes a person to flow in their heavenly language. Fluency in your devotional spiritual language greatly helps you experience and speak with prophetic unction.

2. Acknowledge the Psalm 95:7 nugget: "Today if you will hear His voice."
a.) The hearing of God's voice is largely a matter of will.
b.) This hearing must be a "today" thing that you do.

1. It's all about the Benjamites (2 Chronicles 14:8, 1 Chronicles 12:2). The Benjamites were ambidextrous; they could shoot arrows and hurl stones with either hand. They carried shields and spears, drew bows, and were mighty in valor. You must mirror their versatility in spiritual giftedness. This age calls for evangelistic entrepreneurship; that's why you have it in your heart to do so many things.

Prophetic Evangelism – Field Activation Manual
Scene Study
Fill In the Blanks

Q. 1. What does the "oxen issue" represent in our church services today?

_____
_____
_____
_____

Q. 2. Without the prophetic, our evangelistic programs suffer from the lack of _____ to _____the unchurched.

Q. 3. An evangelist is to be a _____ to the lost and emerging secular culture.

Q. 4. What are three categories of prophetic evangelistic acts mentioned in this chapter?

_____
_____
_____
_____

Q. 5. What did you learn from Pastor Paul Goulet's testimony regarding his church in Las Vegas?

_____
_____
_____
_____

Extensive Scene Study
Bonus Questions

Q. 1. The prophetic and evangelistic flows are working together to _____ and _____.

Q. 2. What is a "nevertheless, at your word" experience?

_____
_____
_____

Q. 3. Why did Paul choose Silas?

_____

_____

_____

_____

Q. 4. Give an example of a dying-to-self abandonment act.

_____

_____

_____

_____

Behind the Scenes
Discussion Questions

Discussion Location: Classroom

1. In evangelism you are a worker together with Christ.
   a. What things can you do in evangelism?
   b. What things can only God do?

2. Our church services must reflect His nature more than our own, but do they?
   a. What in your local church service reflects human nature?
   b. What reflects God's nature?

3. What if prophecy met evangelism?

"The prophetic anointing is able to look into the heart of God, and have the ability to discern the things that the enemy is trying to launch. The anointing of the evangelist has the ability to look into the heart of the lost culture and see a need."
– *Sean Smith*, Prophetic Evangelism

What do prophecy and evangelism work together to do?

4. What does "at Your word" evangelism require of you? Name some examples of "at Your word" evangelism in the Bible and their outcomes.

5. "The important thing is, in every way, that Christ is proclaimed."
   – *Sean Smith*, Prophetic Evangelism

In what ways is Christ not being proclaimed? Talk about any innovative ideas that you might have for evangelism that would benefit unreached people.

Cutting Room Floor
Application

The chapter of Prophetic Evangelism titled "When Prophecy Meets Evangelism" says, "Prophetic evangelists don't rely on their ability to persuade people, they rely on the Holy Spirit to reveal." In this exercise we are going to allow the Holy Spirit to reveal the needs of people in our community. The needs of people in our communities as well as the world have grown. It is up to us as the body of Christ to go out from our pews and into the world where we are called to be witnesses. We can do this by what we refer to as a prayer walk.

In groups of two, ask God to show you an area where the spiritual needs of the people are great. Knock on at least ten doors, asking people what their needs are and if you can pray for them. Allow the Holy Spirit to guide you as you pray. Realize that behind each door, the needs of the people differ. Prepare your hearts and minds to minister to each individual with the wisdom of God.

The Making of an Epic
Journaling

The charges of a prophetic evangelist involve being watchful during afflictions and doing the work of an evangelist.

1. As you have read this chapter, you have seen characteristics of the evangelist and the prophet. You've seen similarities between the anointings; from revelation and insight, to creative powers and change. You have read about the results of prophetic evangelism. With this knowledge in mind, journal a prayer in the spirit of the pastor who prayed in *Prophetic Evangelism*, "God, while I'm down here, why don't you go ahead and do whatever you want to me?"

2. Write an experience where you've been specifically led to share your faith. How did the "leading" come about for you?

44

Journal Notes

Journal Notes

Chapter 4

A Case For A Historic Harvest

There's an end-time harvest coming, the magnitude of which will stagger the average Christian's thinking.

Favorite Scene Selections
Harvest Theology

My favorite scene selection in this chapter is the understanding of the prophetic promises of harvest that God gives us regarding the end-times. The problem for most people is not a lack of social skills, but a lack of God's perspective. **When you meditate upon the coming sovereign move, a certainty rises up in your heart and puts you in the right frame of mind to share your faith**. We have to see the opportunities and the unprecedented; we have to see beyond the obvious.

It has been said that a world view is the interpretive lens through which you perceive life and your world. It becomes your compass arrow and filter that originates and organizes your various views of your life journey.

Statistics bear witness to the fact that thousands of people will reach spiritual turning points in the next 24 hours. Estimates have the number of new religions in North America at somewhere between 700 and 1,000 depending upon how you define "new religions." Forty-four million Americans will heavily invest and become involved in campaigns of spiritual awareness according to a ten-year study reported by Dow Jones and Company. In America alone, 411 people will convert to Islam, 872 will become Mormons, and more than 5,000 will join a church or receive Christian baptism.

According to *Mission Frontiers* magazine, Christianity is growing at the rate of 90,000 new believers everyday worldwide. The Christian population of the world in terms of total adherents is well over one billion people.

In communist China, in the face of sometimes terrifying government opposition, people are committing themselves to a spiritual relationship with Jesus Christ at a rate averaging about 28,000 new converts a day. Latin America witnessed a rise from 50,000 believers in 1900, to estimated figures of over 100 million Christians a hundred years later. I'm encouraged by what God has done in Korea. In the year 1900, Korea had no Protestant church; it was deemed "impossible to penetrate." Today Korea is 35 percent Christian with 7,000 churches in the city of Seoul alone.

Some say that Christianity is on the decline. Not so! It is estimated that of every genuine Christian since the first century, 70 percent had their life-transforming encounter with Jesus since WWII. And of them, 70 percent became Christians in the last 4 to 5 years. God doesn't have geographical favorites per se, but He does honor faith. The unchurched population in the United States is so huge that if it were a nation, it would be the fifth most populated nation on the planet. We must have a fresh vision for the harvest. Once that is in place, God will release His energy, power, and Spirit into you and through you.

The UNCHURCHED *population in the* United States *is so huge that if it were a nation, it would be the* FIFTH MOST POPULATED *nation on the planet.*

Director's Bonus Commentary
The Importance of Faith

The silent discussion we conduct in our heads is crucial. No, you're not the only one who talks to yourself. Faith is embodied when the confidence required to be a witness is experienced as a gift from God. Being a witness is not only an occasion, but also a test of faith. Evangelism always requires faith—we must believe that He desires, more than anything, for the lost to be found. We must have faith that God can use us. We must have faith to discern His voice and go where He leads us. God has miracles in store for you. If we fail to step out in faith, the people who need our ministry will not be touched.

In Mark 11:21-24, Jesus challenged His disciples to have faith in God, and if they didn't doubt but believed the things they said would be done, they would have them. I've often said that lost people were going to get saved or become radical Christians; these faith confessions are important to your long-term success in witnessing.

In America, it takes the combined efforts of 85 Christians working over an entire year to produce one convert. This is a statistic based on numbers, not on effort. It shouldn't take an entire village to see just one salvation over a 12-month span! Jesus cursed a fig tree that had leaves but no fruit! Be determined and committed to have a life that bears fruit. Listening to God must always be accompanied by obedience. **Superficial faith never sees the harvest; only supernatural faith enables a vessel to reap souls.**

I'm not going to waste my life on something that is not miraculous. We must get to the point where we depend on miracles. We must believe in the day-to-day supernatural operation of the Holy Spirit. You were meant to be a vessel for the activity of the Father on the planet, in this epoch. Faith is always the activating force for revelation, not feelings, sensations, or spiritual fleeces. Remember that right perspective is one of the most valuable commodities on the planet. You must carry an elevated atmosphere of anticipation to experience profound expressions of God's power.

Facts on faith:

1. You can't wait to feel faith; faith is not a feeling. Faith is a decision. **We are the offspring of our outlook.** At times your greatest obstacle may not be the one with horns coming out of his head, but the head you face in the mirror every day.

2. We must focus our faith and energy on rescuing souls; begin to believe for an awakening. The promises of God are ammunition in the weapon of a soul warrior.

3. Your intellect and reasoning can be a box of doubt. Whatever you do in this season—walk by explosive faith!

Scripture speaks of the "proportion of faith" (Romans 12:6). It is proportionate to the job at hand linked to the need. Faith produces interaction between you and Christ. If you fail to step out in faith, the people who need your ministry will not be touched. You must be prophetic in your outlook of what God wants to do in your world.

> It is a crime to bend God's exclamation mark into a question mark.
> — Reinhard Bonnke

Each generation of believers must undergo a miracle of discovery. In Luke 4:18-19, Jesus knew what faith promises He had to rightfully declare as being ful-filled in Him. The early Christians knew what their mission was in the world; they defied Satan and ten Roman emperors who had them persecuted, and they still out-lasted them all. **The environment didn't make the early believers—they made the environment.** You too have been chosen to change the atmosphere, and it will take breakthrough faith in a great God! Don't let the thief of unbelief rob you of Christ's current payday of souls.

To experience breakthrough faith, we must be prepared to deal with the obstruc-tions of unbelief. Unbelief has choked and torqued the life out of our faith, espe-cially in the western world. Jesus required faith as small as a mustard seed; the emphasis is on *quality* faith, where God is the originator and manufacturer.

In Mark 9:14-29, the disciples tried unsuccessfully to emancipate and bring light to a demonized boy. This led to a public dispute and armed the enemies of the gospel with arguments. The father of the boy brought his tormented son to Jesus, begging for help. This is the picture of your postmodern world, where a lack of effectiveness has become the number one bullet used against us. Jesus set the boy free and the disciples asked Him privately, "Why could we not cast it out?" Good question! Why couldn't they demonstrate what Christ made available? Jesus' response was simple (Matthew 17:20): unbelief. Why aren't we seeing more of our friends and family set free from unbelief? Maybe it's because we're still fighting a root of it in our own lives.

This word "unbelief" is not just an absence of faith, but resistance to faith. If you are full of faith, your actions will be faith actions. **You can't afford spiritual smugness—to be falsely content with results that are skimpy and sub par because you usually get what you reach for in the kingdom.** Faith is a choice as well as a gift; it's letting God witness your earthly affirmations of His heavenly truth despite your conditions.

In Matthew 16:6, Jesus warned the disciples to "beware of the leaven of the Pharisees and Sadducees." The Pharisees were religious and bound by institutional and traditional agendas. Meanwhile, the Sadducees questioned the spirit realm, disbelieved the transmission of any oral prophecy law by Moses, and rejected the prophets.

The leaven of the Sadducees was skepticism in the supernatural and insecurity with the prophetic. The leaven of the Pharisees was a religious spirit that wanted to be in control and have everything in its airtight, hermetically sealed boxes. They also worshipped their traditions. Often, when Jesus could not perform miracles in the Bible, it was directly related to the mindset of the people in the area who refused to give up their restricting traditions.

Jesus warned His disciples to not give into this "leaven," which would keep them from flowing in the supernatural and bringing the "bread" of life to the masses. I challenge you to take some time and meditate on these passages and pray out of yourself any "leaven." Satan wants to leaven your soul to stop prophetic evangelism from launching out of your spirit. God wants to give your lost world some "unleavened" bread.

There are three zones of faith (Hebrews 10:35-39):

1. Apprehension Zone—you're tentative, it's somewhat awkward. This is where you're uncertain and cautious about the issue.

2. Acclimation Zone—you start getting familiar with something, but you're not quite sure. You're getting a feel for the issue and the seed of faith is beginning to flourish. Faith is a response; you move to God's invitation. A delayed response is usually a display of doubt.

3. Assurance Zone—this is where the issue is settled. Faith is achieved and doubt is suspended. Look out—God will move!

A proper understanding of God's sovereign almightiness assures us that no situation exceeds His reach, no circumstance escapes His attention, and no experience is beyond His control.

Deleted Footage
Devised Means

God not only saves lives, but He also devises means to intervene. You are called to the ultimate cosmic crisis intervention. We must believe that we are God's devised means. We must believe that God has a specific interception plan for every lost soul. The plurality of devised means would infer that the salvation plan involves more than just Jesus doing His job on the cross. You are God's devised means, and you have a job to do, also.

Every single believer has a strategy of heaven on their heads to see the redemption of others. Devised means indicates that God has plans for you to be involved in the divine setup of the life of an unbeliever. **Devised means speaks of the fact that God Himself calculates, invents, and makes custom plans to break into unchurched peoples' worlds to bring them a world of His own.**

God also delights in bringing you into that plan for someone and is in fact making you the plan itself. Your fingerprint is intended to mark some area of the kingdom, and it is impossible to substitute someone else's print or spiritual retina scan for yours. Every passing day might be unfolding a new page of God's redemptive devised means for someone you are being sent to. I'm convinced that God makes, and ensures, multiple approaches into the lives of unbelievers to see them come to the saving knowledge of the Lord Jesus Christ.

Devised defined: "A person who makes plans with the intent of carrying them out, or regards something in a certain way that then affects their actions toward that thing."

Means defined: "Thoughts are translated into action."

The Knox version translates 2 Samuel 14:14 as follows: "He busies Him with remedies to save the life of him who is banished." Make no mistake, God is busy—it's time for you and I to get busy, too! Ephesians 2:10 reminds us that you are God's workmanship, a redemptive product in Jesus the Redeemer's business of soul winning, which has already been laid out before you. As the realization of this truth hits you, faith will arise within you for how much God believes in you in this hour.

I included SIX MYTHS *in Prophetic Evangelism. Now I want to make an addition. The final ultimate myth makeover is* MYTH SEVEN. *You may think to yourself, "If I just live a* GOOD LIFE *in front of the world, it will be sufficient."* BUT NOBODY'S LIFE IS THAT GOOD!

Page 86 of *Prophetic Evangelism* explains that the word *redemption* comes from the Hebrew word meaning "to tear loose and to rescue." You must awaken to your calling to rip the person out of the hold of sin before you rescue him.

I included six myths in *Prophetic Evangelism*. Now I want to make an addition. The final ultimate myth makeover is myth seven. You may think to yourself, "If I jjust live a good life in front of the world, it will be sufficient." But nobody's life is that good!

Alternate Endings
Not Ashamed and Not Taking It For Granted

The first walk-away timeless truth (W.A.T.T.) in this chapter is that you must believe in the mighty liberating power of the gospel. Paul knew the walk-away factor in Romans 1:16 where he called the gospel "the power of God to salvation for everyone who believes." The gospel is the dynamite, and you are the wick. Psalm 46:10 says, "Be still, and know that I am God; I will be exalted among the nations…." This verse lets us in on how this thing will end. God wants to fill you with some divine optimism.

As you step up and step out, you'll see the amazing results of this gospel you believe, and these results will build more faith for the next exploit. Satan is afraid that you'll really see what the gospel is capable of accomplishing. Sometimes you don't know what you've got until you see it squash the opposition. Whatever the problem or the attack, the answer is always the gospel. If you're convinced of that, it will propel you to convince many others as well. Paul said in 2 Timothy 1:12, "I am not ashamed, for I know whom I have believed and am persuaded...." This was the real secret of his dynamic ministry and influence.

The second W.A.T.T. you must understand is to forsake familiarity. Sometimes the longer we've been around the gospel, the greater our propensity is to diminish the Jesus of the Bible until He becomes predictable. In Mark 6, Jesus couldn't perform any mighty work due to Nazareth's hometown familiarity. Familiarity is a spiritual computer virus that will cause your computer mainframe of faith to crash.

It is so crucial in evangelism that the harvest and revival become fresh to you again. Don't fall prey or get the beat down to a defeatist theology that will only feed an isolation spirit. Reject all fear and don't yield to fear for any period of time.

The last W.A.T.T. of this lesson is to dream big in small places. You may be in a big city, big campus, or workplace, yet like the apostles, you must reach your Jerusalem before you reach the uttermost parts of the earth. It's easy to feel like you are in a small place, when you think of the Christian population in comparison to the non-Christian population around you.

Sometimes a prophetic evangelist must fight off a scarcity mentality that says, "You won't affect much" or "create big waves." You have a big destiny, and you must make your dreams match your destiny. **I challenge you today to dream a dream of liberation, of a new ministry flowing through you to a broken world.** Remember, there is an irrevocable connection between how you believe and the action you take.

> If you want to find your ultimate mission field, make sure you are faithful in your immediate mission field.
> —Jim Buchan

Outtakes Countdown

10. Crave to construct a conviction. Natural eyes see problems where spiritual eyes see promises. Only those who live out their conviction can move the masses. We often see great leaders who are gifted in an area and we try to mimic their movement, which typically leads to frustration. You must first possess their revelation to be possessed by their revelation. Remember, a revelation causes a conviction, and a conviction produces movement!

9. Read the stories of successful soul winners and the radical accounts of revivals. This will build your faith that the Holy Spirit will do it again only larger, and through you. What you meditate on will feed your spirit and lead your soul!

8. Have a vision of your harvest and speak your vision consistently. Speaking your vision is incredibly important. It will not only build your faith, but it will help you remember your mission and purpose. Make some prophetic evangelism decrees: "I will win the lost," "I will be a catalyst of revival on my campus and in my community," "I will go the distance...."

7. Get some wins under your belt first. Step into some redemptive opportunities, make them positive, then step aside looking next time to take it to the next level. Stack an outreach in your favor and stack it against the devil. Walk away feeling so excited and unable to wait until the next time you can do some prophetic evangelism.

6. Don't be lax in your La-Z-Boy. Faith is a catalyst; it intensifies your focus. Faith will empower your witness and energize your life. Doing nothing not only robs you of a promised-land blessing, but also saps you of spiritual stamina. Make sure to keep your focus even after establishing some of your bold initiatives.

5. Get out of the world of maybe and into the universe of will be. Double-mindedness is a curse that stops heaven's conveyor belt from the Father to you. Do these three things now: target tenacity, engender enthusiasm, and risk relentlessly. Remember anything that is not faith will be upended and torn down by the tests and trials of life.

4. You won't see how to do it until you see yourself doing it. Faith begins with God's will and purpose being known (2 Peter 3:9). The Father is not willing to lose any battles for souls. You must see yourself flowing in prophetic evangelism, winning in the battle for souls, and witnessing lives changing.

3. Move beyond saving faith to kingdom faith. You must stretch and grow beyond just making it to heaven yourself, to making sure that others do, too. Expect to be blessed so that you can be a major blessing to the nations. God declares your impact even when your spiritual resume doesn't seem to meet the qualifications for the assignment.

2. Let your faith extend beyond your lifetime. Material things are nice, but souls are eternal. Begin to believe God for things that have eternal consequences.

1. Believe that God can start a holy avalanche through you. There is a postulate called the "Butterfly Effect." Those who study science say that a butterfly flapping its wings in Indonesia could cause an avalanche in Antarctica. You are a major part of a spiritual ecosystem. You better recognize the power within you!

Prophetic Evangelism – Field Activation Manual
Scene Study
Fill In the Blanks

Q. 1. The book of Revelation divulges that two sickles are thrust into the earth. One sickle is for _____ and the other for reaping massive worldwide _____.

Q. 2. A true _____ movement is when every aspect of the body of Christ is doing its job to _____ the lost to Jesus Christ.

Q. 3. What are the six myths that need a makeover?
1. The day of mass conversion is _____.
2. Moves of God will only happen in certain _____ locations.
3.) It's too _____ today for anything to change.
4.) The church has already seen its _____ hour.
5.) People are tired of the _____; nobody wants to _____ it.
6.) America isn't a _____ nation anymore.

Extensive Scene Study
Bonus Questions

Q. 1. Outside of Apostle Paul, who would qualify for the most improbable con version in ancient history?

_____
_____
_____
_____

Q. 2. What are the two schools of thought in the current move of God?

_____
_____
_____
_____

Q. 3. What are the myths you believe about evangelism?

_____
_____
_____
_____

Behind the Scenes
Discussion Questions

Discussion Location: Classroom or one of the highest locations in your city. Examples: the Stratosphere, Space Needle, roof of a tall building or parking lot, somewhere that overlooks your entire city. This is your city that you need to believe for.

1. What tough cases are you believing for?

2. What are the biblical results of fasting? How can you incorporate fasting into your life?

3. What is your function as the salt of the earth?

4. The man with the withered arm in Luke 6 had a withered arm because of lack of use, yet Jesus told him to stretch it out. The moment he moved his arm in obedience to reach out, it became fully functioning. Is your outreach arm withered? What are some practical ways you can stretch it out?

5. How many church services, conferences, prayer meetings, Bible studies, etc., have you been to in the last year?
   a. How many people have you witnessed to in the last year?
   b. Are these numbers at least canceling each other out? If there is more coming in than there is going out, you will begin to become a spiritual Dead Sea.

Cutting Room Floor
Application

As *Prophetic Evangelism* states, "Signs from heaven furnish us with prophetic fuel so that we can have courage and spiritual energy to rise up and reap the harvest regardless of the world's condition." We are called to be the salt of the earth. Day of Radicals is a tool that is just that—radical. As we build courage to reap a harvest, it allows us to go into this world and become salt.

Day of Radicals begins with picking locations where people are the most frequently located (for example, airports, restaurants, bus stops, parks, etc.). The purpose of this exercise is to talk to at least three people about Jesus Christ. Each person is sent out and given a certain area to occupy until the objective is complete. We are called to reap a harvest regardless of the world's conditions.

The Making of an Epic
Journaling

1. List some people you consider unsavable. What makes you consider them tough cases?

2. List some opportunities or goals in your ministry, life, and relationships you consider to be lost and gone.

3. Because you believe in the God of resurrection, write down thoughts that show your belief that these people can be saved, and these circumstances can change for the good.

4. Journal a prayer of faith for these people and these circumstances.

Homework Assignment

God wants to rip apart the veil of confusion in your world, your identity, and your image. The bottom line is that you need to realize that in Christ, you're a whole person now. Find a picture that shows who you are now in God.

Journal Notes

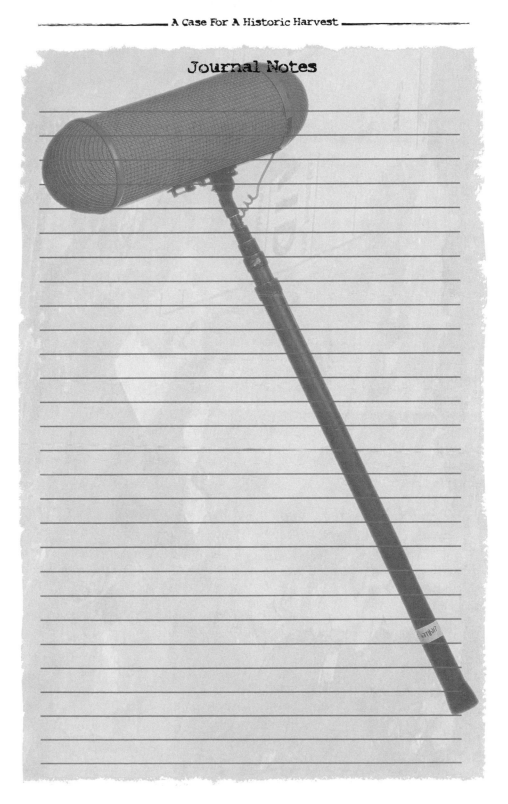

Journal Notes

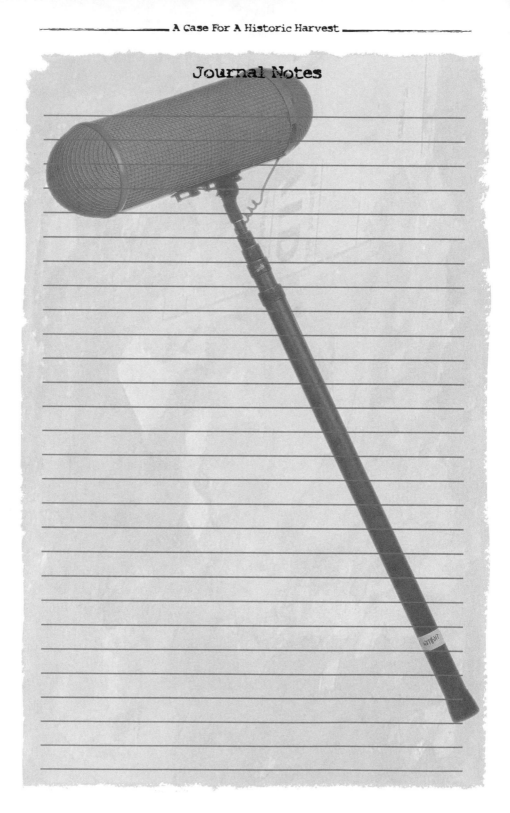

Chapter 5

Brokeness, Boldness, and the "Bless-Me" Mentality

You lose what you don't give away! Begin with your heart.

Favorite Scene Selections
The Compassion of Christ

"Compassion is about aligning your heart with God's. Our Lord is sorrowful for the lost. He misses us. He desperately desires a relationship with us."
– *Michael Simpson*

The New Testament church was continually reaching out. It was continually spilling out, and running into the world around it. **God is raising up a new millennium salvation army that will be carried to the four corners of the globe with a mantle of a broken heart and brokers of supernatural manifestations.** You are the manifestation of God's love on planet earth. The Holy Spirit is inside of you tugging at your heart to see into the hearts of the lost. Compassion is a mind and heart response of openness to God's leading that rises from a personal observation of human need. Compassion leads to a specific action to meet that need.

You've seen movies where producers deliberately try to suck every emotion out of your very being—you laugh, you cry, and everything in between. How is it that you cry and are deeply moved for things that aren't real, yet pass by hurting people and not want to be bothered? **We've become such a dangerously voyeuristic culture through reality TV that we've become numb as a product; we don't feel anymore**. We have video games that make us think we have power in our lives that we don't really have, and that give us the adrenaline rush of fighting evil forces for somebody's freedom. Let's get out of the fantasy realm and get into the reality realm—accept no substitutes! Ask the Lord for the gift of knowing and identifying your community's pain.

Intercession and Intervention

It is significant that the Lord spoke of harvest in the same breath as compassion. Compassion is key to unlocking the end-time harvest. If you love the lost, you will reap the lost. Certain components of Christ's nature must be sown into the hearts of believers to prepare us to carry the anointing for this generation. God will go to great lengths to reach people and captivate hearts. The Holy Spirit will go off the chart to pull people out of darkness.

There is an anointing for miracles contained within compassion. Compassion always releases the hand of the Lord, and purity of heart releases compassion. As it says in Matthew 5:8, "Blessed are the pure in heart for they shall see God." We must open our hearts to flow in Christ's compassion; it is important to realize that we need to be willing to allow the Holy Spirit to prepare us to carry a pure and perfect anointing from the Father.

In Matthew 9:35-38, Jesus demonstrates something so powerful that a department in hell has been set up to blind you to this timeless principle. Jesus, in the midst of carrying on His business, took the time to *see* the people. Once Jesus saw the multitudes, He was hit with a deep yearning in His gut that wrecked Him concerning apathy, passivity, or turning a blind eye towards their violent need of God. This gut-level, deep yearning also caused Him to see them redemptively. Jesus referred to goats as "sheep having no shepherd." Jesus referred to the lost as "pre-believers" needing spiritual guidance.

Divine Intervention

Can you see the tattooed and pierced counter-culture as Christ sees them? Can you see the rich, arrogant yuppie who is fully bank-rolled, yet spiritually fully bankrupt simply as "sheep without a shepherd?" **Sinners aren't the enemy, they're prisoners of the enemy (Colossians 1:13).** If you can't see them in this way, you won't experience the effectiveness as the prophetic evangelist that God has made you. Jesus goes on to say that participating in His heart involves a burden both to pray and to become a laborer for souls.

Divine release comes to those whose hearts beat in rhythm with the human condition and heaven's compassion. The word "burden" actually means "creating a

> They will be men who will preach with broken hearts and tear-filled eyes, and upon whose ministries God will grant an extraordinary effusion of the Holy Spirit and who will witness signs and wonders following in the transformation of multitudes of human lives.
> —*Arnold Dallimore,* George Whitefield: The Life and Times of the Great Evangelist of the Eighteenth Century

sense of responsibility." The good news is that God furnishes those who will take responsibility with divine ability. We need to see people the way God sees people. You can't manufacture love for people in the flesh.

Interestingly, as Jesus was moved with compassion, He stepped into a trigger mechanism for tremendous miracles. *Agape* love is the flash point for a surge of salvation to flow through you. God's heart would beat in our chest, and our lives would move in tune with each beat. **We've been better at articulating the mind of God than at moving in the heart of God.** Understanding God's character and His passion for rescuing the lost is critical to realizing our part in winning the lost. You must spend time with unbelievers and move out of your comfort zone. You must get up close to those who are dead in their trespasses and slaves of darkness. Then you will understand who is before you, and Who they're missing.

Director's Bonus Commentary
Prophetic or Preoccupied

"When people follow Christ, God's priorities become theirs. Therefore, the choice to be involved in reaching friends and relatives is normal for the follower of Christ. Avoidance and disengagement are abnormal."
– *Author Tom Clegg*

Being "prophetic" is often interpreted as predicting the future, which can be a very limited definition of what prophecy is all about. Having heaven's perspective, the Father's heart, and Christ's mission at heart is as prophetic as anyone could ever get. Jesus, in John 4:35-38, reminds us to not dismiss the immediacy of the ripeness of the harvest right beneath our noses. **Being prophetic means recognizing promising opportunities and allowing your heart to flow in symphony with God's heart towards the harvest.** When the eyes of your heart are opened, you become prophetic and you can see what God is pointing out.

"I believe that the greatest obstacle to the evangelization of the world is the Church that is preoccupied with its own existence rather than focused upon Jesus Christ."
– *Author Douglas Ceal*

Jesus is also pointing out the preoccupied, those who are putting off to the future what they should be participating in today. Jesus Himself, the Captain

Being "prophetic" is often interpreted as PREDICTING THE FUTURE, *which can be a very limited definition of what* PROPHECY IS ALL ABOUT.

of our salvation, modeled staying free from preoccupations. The Bible tells us that 1) Jesus came for the lost (Luke 19:10), 2) He came for the sick (Mark 6:5-6), and 3) He came for the oppressed (Matthew 11:28). Jesus stayed true to His assignment although others tried to get Him involved in politics and other distractions (Matthew 22:21).

Jesus emphasizes this point in John 4:35-38 by challenging His disciples not to not delay focusing on the harvest under any circumstances. It is easy for individual Christians and the corporate body of Christ to get sidetracked and make a diversion out of God's blessings.

In modern Christianity, amidst a world turned cold, one of the rarest commodities is real *agape* love. *Agape* is the Greek word for the God kind of love. Maybe the most essential quality one must possess to be effective in prophetic evangelism is a robust love-walk for those separated from the Creator. **True prophecy is utterly incapable of being cold, clinical, or detached. Prophecy must be conceived and delivered in love.** I've seen God use people who were socially challenged but who had a profound love for the lost. In our campus ministry we had a young man who was definitely in the out-crowd (as opposed to in-crowd), but brought more people in the kingdom than other more popular students I knew. His secret was that he cared about people as much as anyone I've ever met. When God can entrust us with His heart, He can trust us with His harvest.

Ironically in Nineveh's awakening, Jonah became useful when God could channel His heart, coupled with His power, through him. Jonah had to let go of his biased human sentiment to see one of the Old Testament's greatest awakenings in a heathen nation. What are some of the things that you must release to reach certain groups around you?

Agape Deficit Disorder can creep into congregations that refuse to reach out to un-churched people who are economically and ethnically different than they are. It also manifests in a Christian hesitancy to reach out to those bound in socially less acceptable sins. Having an equal-opportunity love is key to the magnitude of harvest that God has designated for you in this age.

Being in tune with the Father's heart means that I should have the same concern, compassion, and passion to reach the perishing. **Many times God allows you to feel in your spirit what someone else is experiencing or what the Lord feels for someone to whom we are witnessing.**

This chapter in *Prophetic Evangelism* closes with some thoughts on brokenness. The thought about brokenness opening the door to revelation is critical. Freeing your heart to flow with the Holy Spirit's emotions allows you to more accurately tap into His wisdom. Many times people ask what helps me become sensitive to the Spirit of God. The answer is found in what makes my heart sensitive in general.

Brokenness is exchanging carnal feelings and crusty attitudes; this is done by entering into a realm of the Spirit through heart contrition, humility, and submission before the Lord. When was the last time you truly felt broken before the Lord? What led to this spiritual state for you? When you're broken, God can call out to your spirit and call forth the spirit of the unchurched person. When you feel overwhelmed, remember God is going to help you catch these truths.

Deleted Footage
Consumed Like Cornelius

The miracle of a changed life and a changed eternal address is no joke. There is nothing like seeing a person get delivered from darkness and committing to Christ. I have always been fascinated by the obsessed-with-soul-winning figures from church history; people like D.L. Moody, Rees Howell, Billy Sunday, Charles Finney, Kathryn Kuhlman, and others.

One soul winner whose heart stands out is C.T. Studd. England's golden boy, Studd was the captain of their cricket team and was fairly affluent. Studd gave up cricket and invested his fortune in the kingdom by supporting the outreaches of William Booth, D.L. Moody, and George Mueller's orphanages. Studd lived his personal mission statement: **"If Jesus Christ be God and died for me, no sacrifice I make can be too great for Him."**

Who else stands out in the way of giving their all to win souls? A forerunner of prophetic evangelism was John G. Lake, who was a contemporary of the Azusa Street Revival. He grew up in a home of 16 children. Disease came and took eight of his brothers and sisters. That plight caused Lake to receive the Holy Spirit's emotion of fervent hatred for sickness. As a result, Lake became a man consumed with a passion that became fuel for historic advancements against the devil.

Even as we must receive God's emotion for the unchurched, we must also receive God's emotion against the works of darkness. My hatred of what darkness does to lives also drives me in prophetic evangelism. Lake's burden drove him to see the full release of what Christ died for. The sequence I've seen is that God gives you a revelation that produces a conviction and burden that ultimately release the movement and manifestation. The revelation of Christ as a redeemer and deliverer produces miracles, manifestations, and mass conversions.

If there was ever a consumed vessel in ancient history who modeled what it takes to release a God-awakening, it was Cornelius in Acts 10. Consumed with passion to see a redemptive move amongst his people, Cornelius gave alms and poured out of his heart towards heaven. God is a giver. When you come to an outreach, you must come to give.

Cornelius's whole life was an outpouring of a broken heart that broke through previously brass heavens that was over an outsider people group to the gospel, the Gentiles. Cornelius became a catalyst of redemption for the nations, and his heart left an ascending mark before heaven. An angel even told him that, "your prayers and your alms (offering and gifts) have come up for a memorial before God." Memorials are where history is being made. What are you willing to give so that the spiritually dead may live? As we grow in love for others, we are positioning ourselves to receive revelation from the Holy Spirit. Brokenness allows for a greater capacity of God to be released.

We must be in tune with the Father's heart and plugged into His power; otherwise, we're limited to our own power, evangelizing in the flesh and not in the Spirit (Zechariah 4:6). That is when evangelism becomes a burden rather than a blessing. God wants to replace the grind with some grace. When I speak, nothing happens; when God speaks, the universe comes into existence.

The power is found not in convincing God to my agenda, but in waiting upon Him to hear His agenda. John 2:17 tells us that Jesus was eaten up by zeal for the Father. I want to challenge you to use the 15 key intercessory targets (see *Prophetic Evangelism* pages 94 to 95) to pray continuously over the lost. Prayer draws you not only towards the Father, but also toward those you pray for. Your love walk will take quantum leaps.

I am absolutely convinced the power of heaven is unlocked on earth when we devote ourselves to the secret place. **The body of Christ is not a social club; it is a war room, advancing to take new territory.** Prayer gives you a fresh sense of the purpose of God for your life.

Alternate Endings
All for the Kingdom

The first walk-away timeless truth (W.A.T.T.) of this chapter is simple, yet profoundly necessary. This chapter is meant to create in you a kingdom heart, which is a passion for experiencing and expanding the kingdom. There is a definite need for us to get in touch with the kingdom heart. Jesus said the kingdom of God is a treasure so valuable that we should be willing to sell everything we have to obtain it. A kingdom heart beats for kingdom fruit. It beats to liberate those who are in bondage to the powers of darkness. As Christians, we need a kingdom heart to impact the world with the gospel. In the western world, we are constantly bombarded by a fury of our culture's attitude and values.

W.A.T.T. number two is simply that history belongs to the intercessor. Samuel Chadwick gave this warning to Christians who work but don't pray: "The one concern of the devil is to keep the saints from praying. He fears nothing from prayerless work, prayerless religion. He laughs at our toil, he mocks at our wisdom, but he trembles when we pray." E.M. Bounds once said, "The Church on its knees would bring heaven upon the earth."

God opens the heavens and removes mountains for the intercessor. Sometimes we miss out because we haven't "prayed the price." Jesus said, "My house shall be called a house of prayer for all nations" (Mark 11:17). As prophetic evangelists, you must speak to God on behalf of the oppressed and captive.

In the late 1990's, 154,000 Protestant churches reported no conversions. This shows a disinterest or lack of passion for reaching the lost. Bishop Vaughn McLaughlin says, "You won't be successful doing what God told you to do—you will be successful doing what God is telling you to do." **This principle tells you that to be successful, you must not just be moved with compassion, but keep moving with compassion.**

You must spend time with unbelievers and get up close to those who are "dead in trespasses." Then you'll gain in compassion. Love is the flash point for surges of salvation to flow through you. Moving in compassion will facilitate your prophetic evangelism flow. True prophecy and evangelism is utterly incapable of being cold, clinical, dispassionate, and detached. Prophecy must be conceived and delivered in love. The essence of biblical evangelism comes down to being in tune with the Father's heart. Even though unbelievers may turn their backs, you don't have license to turn your heart.

Outtakes Countdown

10. Forsake the luxury of being unmoved around a crowd ever again. Jesus was always moved with compassion. Compassion wants to transport you someplace in the Spirit, if you'll let it. Put all your emotional chips in the middle of the table and go for broke when you're in the masses of lost humanity.

9. Remember that miracles and conversions begin where the "bless me" mentality ends. Move away from Christianity 101A, which is when believers desire more presents from heaven with their name on the package. Point the arrow (your heart focus) outward rather than inward. Begin to pray and fast like you've never prayed and fasted before. Begin to believe for God's kingdom to come to needy individuals.

8. Eliminate the numbing influences in your life. Get rid of any sensual Novocain; it will only deaden your spirit, and in the words of Mel Gibson's William Wallace, "dim your wit." Take a spiritual inventory of your life in this season.

7. Prepare your heart for witnessing as much, or more than, you prepare your words to share. The right words will have the right effect when they come out of the right heart (Matthew 12:34). God graces a prepared heart with phenomenal insight and wisdom.

6. Read the crucifixion; see *The Passion of the Christ*. You must allow Jesus's life and movement to speak to your life in an ongoing fashion. In this process Jesus will begin His movement in and through you.

5. Determine not to get stuck condemning the already condemned. Jesus came not only to give them a break, but also to rescue them. If you're going to bust someone out of prison, why complain about his cell?

4. Put yourself in a burden-stirring situation. Don't avoid the needy areas and people in your city; they have a role in who God is making you to be; they have the yoke that activates your anointing.

3. See the faces, hear the cries. It always helps to personalize the oppressed. A sociopath can only victimize people whom they have dehumanized in their thinking. You must be the anti-sociopath and see God's fingerprints on every soul.

2. Make a list of unsaved people whom you want to reach with God's love. Write it up now! Don't wait! We've waited long enough!

1. Seek to pick up the mantle of a tender heart. King Josiah had a tender heart that attracted mercy (2 Kings 22:19, 2 Chronicles 34:27). My son's middle name is Josiah for this reason. Pray for the spirit of Josiah to tenderize your heart.

Prophetic Evangelism – Field Activation Manual
Scene Study
Fill In the Blanks

Q. 1. The _____ is nothing less than what saves a _____.

Q. 2. Our assignment is to love people enough to endure the _____
that stand in the way of their _____.

Q. 3. Define a burden.

_____

_____

_____

_____

Q. 4. What are the five attributes of a burden?
   a. A burden is spiritual _____.
   b. A burden is of _____origin.
   c. A burden is_____unique.
   d. A burden is deeply _____.
   e. A burden makes you_____.

Q. 5._____ is about understanding lost people and loving lost
people by giving them _____ to God.

Q. 6. What Bible character had the Agape Deficit Disorder?

_____

_____

_____

_____

Q. 7. What three things does brokenness do?

_____

_____

_____

_____

Q. 8. Prophetic evangelism is about _____ touching _____.

Extensive Scene Study
Bonus Questions

Q. 1. What did Aaron do that stopped the plague?

_____

_____

_____

_____

Q. 2. Before evangelism is a program, it is a _____.

Q. 3. What is the "Jonah Syndrome"?

_____

_____

_____

_____

Q. 4. Today's ___ _____makes tomorrow's _____ possible.

Behind the Scenes
Discussion Questions

Discussion Location: Unfamiliar place. Before you begin your teaching, you must select a location. While determining your location, keep in mind that you are teaching about the lost people of this world. To illustrate this point, you should look for places around your local area that seem to be desolate or abandoned. It needs to be a place where once your students arrive, they will have no idea where they are; they're lost.

Once you have selected your location, on the day of the teaching start by informing your students that they are about to be a part of an illustrated teaching. Next you will have to place a leader in each car well prepared to arrive at the destination. Blindfold the students and instruct them to not remove their blindfolds until they are told to do so.

Upon their arrival at the destination site, the students should have no idea where they are located. This will give you the ideal atmosphere for teaching what the lost feel like without Jesus Christ in their lives.

1. Do you have any close friends or relatives who could be described as a lost person? Describe their relationship with you.

71

2. Talk about some reasons why you can be heartbroken for humanity.
   a.) Discuss specific people groups, fads, phenomena, and disasters. Get in touch with your heart for lost souls.
   b.) How can you stand in the gap for the people just mentioned?

3. The book uses the phrase "the sabotage of a burden" as being distracted by entertainment or personal goals. What are some distractions keeping you from God's burden?

4. What are the ways our culture worships convenience?

5. The adversary to loving lost humanity is a judgmental, condemning attitude; how do we deal with the things that offend us and still love lost humanity?

6. We have read that revelations can motivate you for soul winning. How does a revelation of hell motivate you to reach the lost people? How does a revelation of rewards motivate you to reach lost people?

7. Why is it so important to be broken?

Cutting Room Floor
Application

Play the DVD provided in this workbook. As they see the faces on the DVD, have each person begin to pray, asking God to make a difference in what they see on the screen. This prayer DVD causes us to see life differently; our prayer can go in and make a difference.

The Making of an Epic
Journaling

1. Write a prayer for a lost soul in your life. Use your understanding and the "15 Key Intercessory Targets" from *Prophetic Evangelism* to help in this journaling project.

2. What emotions or burdens did you feel as you wrote your prayer?

Journal Notes

Journal Notes

Chapter 6

The Weaponry Of A Spiritual Freedom Fighter

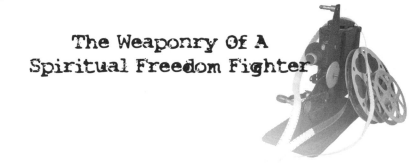

If you think Christianity is like a war, you will only be "like" prepared for the battle.

"I am as safe on the battlefield as I am in my own bed."
–*Stonewall Jackson*

Favorite Scene Selections
Negotiating the Obstacle Course—
Battleground vs. Holy Ground

This chapter begins with the statement, "If you're going to win souls, you're going to have to war." Like they say in the inner city, "Don't bring that Kool-Aid to a gym party." In other words, you must bring the appropriate apparatus to match your cnvironment; you must bring heavy-duty artillery for the heavy-duty battle for souls.

My favorite scene in this chapter is "Negotiating the Obstacle Course." The Bible is clear that the closer we get to Jesus' return, the more intense our spiritual battles will become (Revelations 12:17 and 2 Timothy 3:1).

Anytime you set out to become a fiery witness, you will come up against an Elymas spirit (Acts 13). Initially, this spirit will oppose you, resist you, and cause you to feel unsuccessful in your attempts to evangelize. This spirit wants your resignation; this spirit wants you to sign your walking papers.

Secondarily, this spirit releases a darkening mist that clouds those whom we're witnessing to, making it difficult for them to hear what we're saying. My choice for a militaristic theme for this chapter is purposeful and prophetic. We are in a seriously contested battlefield in our world today. Our success depends on our learning curve for battle and our tenacity! If you don't want the beat down, you must learn from the school of hard knocks and fight through. As you fight through, God will deposit in you what you'll need for the next season.

Page 104 in *Prophetic Evangelism* mentions that Paul not only encountered obstacles, he expected them. Elymas, the sorcerer who resisted Paul, is a modern-day spirit that is an assassin. He comes to kill your witness and take out your clarity. Many times would-be prophetic evangelists don't prepare themselves for resistance and fade to oblivion when the heat is on. God wants to toughen you up like a prizefighter of old to sucker-punch secularism and upper cut any obstacle to secure souls. There is a reason why you're faced with so much warfare over your call. Each battle takes you higher; each conquest makes you hungrier.

Jesus emphasizes the proper attitude in taking kingdom territory in Matthew

> *There is a reason why you're faced with so much* **WARFARE OVER YOUR CALL.** *Each battle takes you higher; each* **CONQUEST** *makes you hungrier.*

11:12, where He states for time and eternity that the kingdom of heaven suffers violence and the violent take it by force. Forceful people won't take "no" for an answer. **Being forceful isn't always being bull-headed and bulldozing. It's being resolute to fight through even the Christian crowd and scenery to get to the needy spots**. If the devil can dissuade you or deflect you from soul winning, he will.

The only thing the devil understands is greater force. This strong man gives way when the One who is stronger comes on the parking lot (Luke 11:21-22). The devil will listen to you only if you allow the greater One to rise up within you. The first thing you fight during an outreach is a force. The force is all it takes for some people to go home. The force meets you before the people do. It can make you leave feeling defeated.

What are some of the forces that face you? A voracious appetite for souls and an aggressive loving God moving toward those souls bring about a hurricane effect that nothing can stop. Demons, vacillating hypocrites, and mediocre naysayers will be trampled by the inevitable stampede of witnessing warriors whom God is releasing. **The key to negotiating the obstacle course is found in touching Jesus on a continual basis.** If you don't negotiate the obstacle course, you'll end up negotiating a settlement and then calling it freedom.

Battleground versus holy ground is determined by finding the balance between rupturing dark powers and resting in His presence. The battleground is where we contest for souls and fight off the devil's attacks associated with prophetic evangelism. This can wear a vessel down. The holy ground is where we get a Holy

Ghost pit stop and receive strength in God's presence (Isaiah 40:31). You must soak in His omnipotence to soar past hell's obstacles.

Possessing Versus Owning

Let's briefly cover the difference between possession and ownership (Mark 4). When God gives you something, you are only a possessor until you can hold onto it after the devourer's attempt to take it. Then you become an owner (Genesis 15:11).

Acts 14:2-3
But the unbelieving Jews stirred up the Gentiles and poisoned their minds against the brethren. 3 Therefore they stayed there a long time, speaking boldly in the Lord, who was bearing witness to the word of His grace, granting signs and wonders to be done by their hands.

You would think that in the midst of poisoned minds, you would leave it alone and drop it like it's hot! Yet this fiery apostle, like a good fighter, wasn't going to take a fall, and neither should you!

In the midst of opposition Paul remained, ministered, and witnessed a miraculous release. In a hostage situation, a law enforcer must place himself in a position that is often threatening. To see a hostage's deliverance, negotiators have to place themselves in contradictory environments.

In Matthew 10:16, Jesus told the disciples that He sent them out as "sheep in the midst of wolves." The point is that you will incur conflict whenever God sends you out on assignment. In the natural, sheep are on the lower end of the food chain than wolves, yet sheep led by the Lion of the tribe of Judah can beat down wolves led by a serpent.

Director's Bonus Commentary
Using Weapons of Spiritual Mass Destruction and Breaking Spiritual Falsehood

As we've moved through human history, we've become more high-tech and innovative, and we have experienced scientific breakthroughs that have altered our lives permanently. Whereas at one time wars were fought by hand-to-hand combat, now it's all about aerial attacks with missiles, nuclear bombs, and chemical warfare. The talk today is about "weapons of mass destruction" that pose a global threat from which there is no return.

I believe that the body of Christ will make spiritual breakthroughs far beyond the understanding or natural intellect. As this is true in the natural, so it is in the spiritual. We have turned a corner in the eternal scheme of things, where darkness has engineered spiritual weapons—"big guns" that have global spiritual destruction written all over them. Yet God also has His end-time big guns—you and me.

Soldiers train for battle using the surroundings of real battle. When we train troops, we can't just practice on other believers. No, let's take it to the streets! When a gun is loaded with blanks, the bang and recoil is similar to live ammunition. Yet the dummy ammunition makes no mark in the target, because it never reaches it. Live ammunition can hit its mark. You are God's live ammunition to see a generation liberated by the gospel you possess. **Preaching the gospel is warfare; it dislodges the powers of darkness. The proclamation of Christ attacks the evil ideas and dark philosophies of society.** You can't just stand there in war with a loaded weapon—you have to fire. You have to pull the trigger and fire.

An effective battle for souls is a strategy to concentrate evangelism efforts with those who are most receptive. It involves employing a strategy, not just indiscriminately shooting our guns at anything that moves. There are certain targets (unchurched people) who have had their defenses reduced and are vulnerable to the gospel.

"Coming out with the big guns" implies finding the relevant battlefields and meaningful targets. God uniquely places you among a network of relationships on purpose; you must strategically redeem your opportunities with the unreached. Ask yourself, "What are the meaningful targets God has given me?" Church growth expert Donald McGavran says, "Growing churches grow because they recognize the social realities, devise a strategy accordingly, and teach it to their members."

Here are some key essentials:

1. We must have the smarts to know where we're dumb. Admit that we should be continually seeking to grow in our "fishing" techniques.

2. We must know our artillery and armory. A good soldier is competent with his gun and supplies. He can assemble it in the dark, if necessary. Our present darkness is no excuse for spiritual disorientation or passivity.

3. We must be familiar with our battle plan. You need to know not only God's plan of salvation, but also God's specific plan for that person's conversion.

"The retreat of the Church has reached its limit. Now the advance will begin; it will gain momentum until the whole world takes notice."
– *Rick Joyner*

The day is over where we can have the luxury of taking or leaving the miraculous. You and your world desperately need God's holy paranormal activities. You can't cut iron handcuffs with paper scissors; neither can you break spiritual falsehood with humanistic sound bites.

Unfortunately, many believers have lost the sense of interplay between the natural and spiritual worlds. The body of Christ has entered into an age of spiritual confrontation and militancy—the struggle between light and darkness will escalate. Our adversary will not willingly hand over his influence on earth without a fight. Redemption was purchased by violence. As in all wars, freedoms are acquired at a cost; someone must rise up to pay the price. These realities will be gained through battles and some agony.

1 John 3:8 tells us that the Son of God was manifested that He might destroy the works of the enemy. Manifestations of the Spirit are meant to destroy the dark works of falsehood.

Deleted Footage
Rising Up to the Occasion

In war, many times an enemy will use propaganda to dishearten his adversaries. Propaganda is the spreading of ideas and information for the purpose of injuring an institution, cause, or person. Propaganda is a tactic employed by the enemy to break the spirit of prophetic evangelism!

Two modern deceptions center on the modern straight jacket of new toleration and the politically correct agenda. New toleration says, "Every philosophy and belief must be equally considered and even accepted." The politically correct agenda says, "You can't be dogmatic and say that there is only one truth." Identifying the lies and deceptive notions the enemy specifically tries to float past you is so crucial.

It is critical in the battle for souls that you maintain your courage. There is momentary courage and momentous courage. **Momentary courage motivates you to perform a one-time act; momentous courage empowers you to respond continuously to help others, day in and day out.**

Prophetic evangelists must know what their trip wires are, and what their trigger points are. Trip wires are the vulnerable explosive areas like land mines in our lives where the enemy most often trips us up. **Heaven doesn't want you to be a casualty of war, another soldier fallen to enemy fire.** I've seen too many Christians fall into immorality and indiscretions. So we must be alert as prophetic evangelists.

Trigger points are the instruments, morale boosters God uses to motivate us and get us up in our lives. Find the catalysts God uses in your life to get you stoked in Jesus. Great leaders of war realize the importance of keeping the morale of the soldiers high; a motivated soldier who is consistently refueled with inspiration contends more enthusiastically in battle.

Psalm 78:9 presents a sad description of a tribe of Israel. The children of Ephraim were equipped for battle but became alarmed in battle and pitifully retreated. Additionally, Hosea 7:8 says that Ephraim was a "cake unturned," meaning they were half-baked followers of the Lord. In the war for souls today, we must deal with any internal issues that could cause us to frazzle in the midst of battle. We have got to be battle-tested and courageous enough to engage the enemy for the release of souls. If you lack spiritual mettle (staying quality, strength of spirit), allow the Holy Spirit to foment a fighter's spirit within you. **We can't be found busy tied up by activities that can't take us to victory.** We can't be attached to tactics that are out of touch with the current threats.

The single most important quality a soldier has is the will to attack. Modern Christians seem to have forgotten the art of contending. We give up after the first resistance. In Jeremiah 51:20-23, God prophesied to Jeremiah and declared the prophet to be His "battle-axe" and "weapon of war." Then the Lord declared His intent to destroy the kingdoms and break into pieces anything and anyone who stood in the way of His plan of redemption.

You must find out what kind of weapon you're meant to be and seek to become that weapon. I wrote this chapter with that revelation in mind. I want to encourage you in this lesson that God wants to use you. Prophetic evangelism is not beyond you, and it's not someone else's job—you are God's warrior for your generation.

> Failure is but a paragraph in the book of each human life. It is the pages that follow that ultimately define us.
> —Colonel Jeff O Lear

"Champions are not made in the ring; they are only recognized there."
– *Joe Frazier*

Alternate Endings
Taking Spiritual Territory

Our first walk-away timeless truth (W.A.T.T.) is learning how to be spiritually violent and how to develop a contending spirit. The body of Christ is not and should not be a social club; it is a war room! Our goal is twofold: 1) We are to hold the ground that God has given us; 2) we are to contend to see the retreating of the kingdom of darkness (you must advance to take new territory). You must walk away from this lesson with a fighter's mentality.

Jesus underscores this W.A.T.T. (in Matthew 11:12) by saying that "the violent take it (the kingdom of God) by force." In other words, spiritual territory will not go to the spiritually passive. **You can't stand there in war with a loaded weapon; you have to fire. You have to decide to discharge your weapon.**

In the Old Testament, a curse was placed upon a village of people by the Angel of the Lord, due to their lack of heart (Judges 5:23). Meroz had the enemy under their feet yet they didn't stomp out their power. Meroz means "secret" and "leanness," which represent the opposite of a fighter's spirit. It is a sympathetic spirit that co-exists with the enemy and its influence. The lesson here is I would rather have the enemy curse me because I challenged darkness than have God curse me because I did nothing and chose the path of least resistance. History has no record of the existence of Meroz; the curse wiped it off the map. Today God wants to put you on the map as you contend for souls.

The second W.A.T.T. is for you to understand the three postures concerning war: evade, pervade, or invade. Evade means to avoid fulfilling, answering, or performing duties. It is the escapist mentality that runs from the battle. The pervade segment of the body of Christ seeks to legislate and use political sticks to hammer out our points. Although I believe that we must seek all available avenues to promote righteousness, these avenues must be secondary to winning souls to Christ. You can enforce laws, but you can't legislate God. Finally, the invade group seeks to penetrate the territory of darkness with the light of the gospel and refuses to sit back quietly.

Friend, make sure you determine to increase in "stickability," or the ability to endure despite hardships and absence of desired results. Jesus said, "My food is to do the will of Him who sent Me, and to finish His work" (John 4:34); this is the original "will work for food!" The pleasure of Christ is the will of God and its execution and fulfillment. Food is what sustains us and is assimilated into the building material of our bodies. If you will stick to God's plan for redemption and see it through, you will be sustained and built up, big time!

Outtakes Countdown

10. "Give me that old-time vigilante Christianity." Many of the saints gone by knew how to lock horns with the enemy and how to get a hold of God. They knew the forgotten phrase "travail and prevail." They got down and dirty in prayer. Somebody needs to tell the devil, "if it's a fight you want, then it's a fight you'll get!" (1 Timothy 6:12)

9. You must have a lock and load mentality. Cultivate a fighter's spirit, refusing to allow obstacles and opposition to stop you. History tells us that in Normandy during World War II, many soldiers never fired their weapons against the enemy because they never even saw them coming. You can't allow that to happen in this crucial war for the minds and hearts of this generation.

8. Be proactive about your perspective (2 Corinthians 4:17-18). In spiritual warfare, perspective is 90 percent of the battle. Especially in prophetic evangelism endeavors, you must guard your outlook, not allowing discouragement or disillusionment to creep in and corrupt. This is always where Satan targets, but he will lose.

7. Be prepared for the battle's backlash. In *Star Wars*, the empire strikes back! Being ready keeps you from being caught off-guard. Become vulnerable before captives, yet invincible before their captor.

6. Bid farewell to a neutral stance and an easy life. It's time to break the unspoken neutrality with the devil. No more, "I'll leave you alone if you'll leave me alone." You have been drafted and given a uniform and weapons; now you must fight. Make no mistake about it—you must hate what the devil does to young people and families. "In each generation, God creates a mysterious trigger that once pulled, blasts a hole in the very core of the evil one's activity." – *Mario Murillo*

5. Fully use the dynamic of the prophetic to wage the good warfare (1 Timothy 1:18). You will grow in your ability to wage good warfare as you implement God's prophetic artillery. When God speaks, the devil is silenced and so is his activity.

4. Watch your morale in the midst of the battle (Nehemiah 8:10). You must keep your joy and make God Himself your source of pleasure. Don't be seduced into going to the enemy for your pleasures; he has traps waiting for you behind his counterfeit pleasures.

3. Contend in private prayer before you contend in public witnessing. You will have more success if you win the battle before going to collect the spoils. It is mighty hard to fight two battles at the same time.

2. See yourself as a deliverer of hostages and a rescuer of kidnapped royalty. It is important for you to visualize and realize these mission assignments. As you do, you will become an emancipator. You cannot impart what you aren't. In other words, if you aren't authentic in living as a liberator of captives, liberty won't flow through you properly.

1. Tolerate no spiritual terrorism. Remember at this moment you are either an available target or an available weapon. Don't let oppression have its way in any life that you can impact. No retreats, no returns, no regrets!

Prophetic Evangelism – Field Activation Manual
Scene Study
Fill In the Blanks

Q. 1. What are two consequences of not knowing how to properly channel the Spirit?

a. We are not seeing an _____, _____ people as God designed us to be.

b. We are not attracting the _____ attention because we appear too often to live a _____ to our message.

Q. 2. Where was Paul sent for his first missionary trip?

_____

_____

Q. 3. What was the Elymas spirit?

a. Elymas was _____ in the art of _____.

b. Elymas was a _____ to the gift of prophecy.

Q. 4. Everybody in the coming age of contending for souls will be filled with something. True   False?

Q. 5. You cannot penetrate a spiritual _____ with _____ weapons.

Extensive Scene Study
Bonus Questions

Q. 1. Paul had the gift of discernment when dealing with Elymas. What is the gift of discernment?

_____

_____

_____

Q. 2. There's a spirit upon _____ _____ that is able to put a dark spin and prejudice in the taste buds of a generation.

Q. 3. How can you break fear and nervousness when attempting to witness?

_____

_____

_____

Behind the Scenes
Discussion Questions

Discussion Location: Classroom

1. What do you call yourself?
   a. Are you functioning in that title?
   b. How can you better function in that title?

2. What was the last real miracle you've seen?
   a. How long has it been since you've prayed for a miracle?
   b. Does anyone need to pray for a miracle right now?

3. *Prophetic Evangelism* lists five points of how people resist the power of the Spirit. The five points are fear, being misunderstood, discouragement, doubt and unbelief, and the devil. Talk about each one, and how it has brought resistance in your life. Have any one of these points allowed resistance to win in you?

4. William Booth said, "If every Christian could taste hell for 30 minutes, it would be good." Combine in your imagination, along with biblical descriptions, what a taste of hell would be like.

5. If your prayer life became more disciplined today, how would it affect life in general (people you love, family, job, etc.)?

6. *Prophetic Evangelism* states, "While Satan is fashioning weapons against us, God is fashioning a defense for us, fashioning you and I into a weapon of choice against the current darkness." If you're the weapon in God's hand, name one thing He's fashioned in you to make you stronger.

7. John G. Lakes once said, "Christianity is 100 percent supernatural." Is this true? How?

8. What are your insufficiencies/weaknesses?
   How will God's sufficiency/strength cover you in your weakness?

Cutting Room Floor
Application

The application of this chapter comes with finding a stronghold, a place where everything is allowed. Some would call it neutral ground, but it's definitely being vied for on a constant basis.

Many of these places include public places where God is not supreme, but it's not totally consumed by Satan. A Greyhound bus station is a great place to feel this oppressive state. Other options are new age book stores, cafés, abortion clinics, college campuses, parks where homeless live and many rejected people gather, and various shelters that are not Christian-based.

You need to discover these areas within your city. You need to find a place where the war is constantly subtle, yet ongoing. Go to an "anything goes" place that looks clean, but really has a spiritual contingency vying for it. Go to that place in groups of two or three, and answer the questions listed in "The Making of an Epic" below. As you are writing, if God gives you the opportunity, and the Holy Spirit prompts you to a person, don't be ashamed and take the opportunity to speak to that person.

The Making of an Epic
Journaling

1. Write a description of your life, with all the oppression you've faced, or write about what your life would have been like had you not been brought up in the truth. Look around you as you write this, and see yourself in the people in the room.

2. Journal a prayer for fresh empowerment of the Holy Spirit in your life.

Journal Notes

Journal Notes

Chapter 7

The DNA Of A Soul Winning Forerunner

You have the opportunity to redefine Christianity to the emerging generation.

Favorite Scene Selections
Lifeless Staffs Versus Prophetic Touch

My favorite section in this chapter is "No More Lifeless Staffs." In 2 Kings 4:31-35, Elisha initially sent his staff with his servant, Gehazi, to bring life to a dead child. This approach failed miserably. It wasn't all Gehazi's fault; he was just mimicking what he had been taught.

My experience tells me that effective evangelism is not about techniques, systems, and methods—it's not about working it out. **Effective evangelism comes from the overflow of a life saturated by the Spirit of God.** Many unsuccessful attempts at awakening the soul of individuals have followed a regimented formula. First of all, we have no indication that Gehazi sought God or was anointed for the task.

Prophetic evangelists must have the following:

1. Prophetic evangelists have an inner history with God where they've made well-worn paths frequently to Him in their past. You must acknowledge and activate the anointing of God on your life.

2. Prophetic evangelists must be confident that there is more at work in their lives than just their own natural strength. When you learn to yield to the anointing, you then release the anointing that you have. Like Jesus, you must boldly declare what the anointing on your life is there to do (Luke 4:18-19). You are God's delivery system, heaven's means of distribution.

3. Prophetic evangelists are people of revelation; they have insight from heaven and expect God to reveal things to them. When Gehazi laid the staff on the dead child, there was neither "voice nor hearing."

First of all, prophetic evangelism is about influence. The spirit of a person influences the people around them. **The presence of God upon an individual triggers certain thoughts in the mind of others.** Second of all, I don't know that Gehazi was convinced of the final result. You must see it, before you really see it! God isn't surprised when His word comes to pass. In prayer, God will let you see things that you'll see with your natural eyes later. For Jesus the activities of heaven seemed as real as the activities of earth. We need to discover Jesus' world view. Things don't necessarily happen when we speak; things happen when God speaks through us.

Finally, I believe that the staff (the impersonal approach) wasn't going to work because Elisha himself (the prophetic) was needed. The "staff" approach is like the phone company that tells you, "Long distance is the next best thing to being there." No! There is no substitute to being there for people. Distance is dead; there will be no impact without contact. Elisha went himself and lay out on the boy 1) mouth to mouth, 2) eye to eye, and 3) hand to hand. This represents the need to 1) speak their language, 2) see from their perspective and view their world, and 3) feel what they are feeling. Even after doing this, the child only became warm, but did not awaken. Remember, when the kid died, he lost his warmth. You may be called to cold situations where you may have to heat things up to pull life back into the situation.

Sometimes people have to warm up to you and the gospel. The staff approach doesn't take into account that there may be a need for warm-ups before people open up to you and your testimony. Elisha stuck with the mission and prayed even more. The child sneezed seven times and came back from the dead. Elisha contended for the supernatural, and so must you.

Get honest with the Lord and admit your need of His power, strength, and anointing in your life. Read through the four gospels and the book of Acts and resolve to do what they say to do. In preparation, before witnessing to others, remind yourself of who Jesus is and seek to empty yourself of self. **God wants to hand you out as a living tract to the masses.**

Director's Bonus Commentary
The Prophetic Anointing—Mt. Carmel Culture

When it comes to the prophetic, we must export the environment and export the experience outside the church walls. That's what Elijah the prophet was directed to do in 1 Kings 18:1-4. God told Elijah that if he would manifest himself before the wicked King Ahab, then He would send rain.

We are looking for safe places while God is looking for leaders who will go into dangerous places. **Ministering as opportunity surrounds us doesn't mean selecting our surroundings, it means maximizing the environment that the Holy Spirit engineers for us.** King Ahab and his wife Jezebel were holding the nation of Israel in captivity to idolatry and deception. A true prophetic evangelist seeks to confront the ungodly systems that hold people in bondage.

Historically, God opens the heavens and pours out blessings when His people go public with righteousness. In the fourth verse, the passage declares that the prophets hid in caves. There will always be a temptation to deactivate and succumb to the politically correct spirit that attempts to dictate your status to "sidelined." A depleted spiritual immune system, due to a lack of devotion, leaves one vulnerable to fear.

Historically, God opens the HEAVENS AND POURS *out blessings when* HIS *people* GO PUBLIC WITH RIGHTEOUSNESS.

In every generation and in every city, there is a battle between the policy and the prophecy. Policies instituted by the spirit of the age rule until followers of Christ manifest the word of the Lord, activating the prophecy over their area. Ahab and Jezebel elevated a cult belief to a national religion status. They set up false prophets and priests while systematically seeking to overthrow the altars of God everywhere. Your day has witnessed a dramatic increase in spiritual experimentation as people draw on many sources to have a do-it-yourself religion. We must see the Church transition adequately to answer this.

The Elijah anointing is one that operates openly in public display. This anointing confronts and challenges darkness.

This anointing:
1. Enables a prophetic people to tackle false spiritual influences
2. Is not intimidated by numbers or popularity
3. Manifests in the bleakest situations
4. Maintains its focus when all the marbles are on the line

Learning how to operate in the anointing of God and recognizing when God's presence is there for a purpose is crucial. We must rediscover the power of the gospel, especially when the heat is on. It's truly getting hot in here and in our nation!

91

What does this mean for you? Elijah came on the scene seeking to convince, through his words, the double-minded masses to serve God alone, and they didn't answer him a single word. Imagine the great, venerated prophet Elijah being ignored. This same overwhelming disregard of our gospel is repeated on a daily basis. Give Elijah some credit; he didn't tuck his tail between his legs and quit. What Elijah did next is epic and vital: he called for a demonstration; he dropped the calling card of the gospel—the supernatural—on the crowd. It's time for the outrageous of God; it's time for outrageous expectations and outrageous exploits. Elijah went to Baal's (Jezebel's idol) home court (Mt. Carmel) and used its supposed signature move (calling down fire) against him.

You as a prophetic evangelist must rebuild the altars of your generation and begin to call for the answer of fire, which will convince the unconvinced. We need the manifestations of God. **We are all for being relevant, yet in adapting to cultural change we must be careful to keep the power of the Spirit and the integrity of the gospel message.** Before moving out of this section, I want to share with you the twin dangers of our culture.

Privatization is the temptation to keep all of our principles and practices in a separate box. Some would call this disconnection, but God calls it denial. The enemy wants you to compartmentalize your faith and just pull it out on Sundays.

Pluralization is the temptation to accept so many choices and options that you can't make any decisions. Some would call this being open-minded; God calls this being carnally minded.

The caved-in prophets symbolized privatization, and the vacillating Israelites that wouldn't answer Elijah symbolized pluralization. Prophetic evangelists avoid both traps and unleash their DNA by challenging folks to press their opinions to practical expression.

The prophetic word has a dynamic ability to PENETRATE THE FALSE *defenses of the intellect. Prophetic words usher forth a strong sense of* GOD'S PROXIMITY *so that the non-Christian experiences what we are describing.*

The prophetic word has a dynamic ability to penetrate the false defenses of the intellect. Prophetic words usher forth a strong sense of God's proximity so that the non-Christian experiences what we are describing. The key to Elijah seeing his nation turn back to God is found in 1 Kings 18:36, which reads, "Lord...I have done all these things at your word."

Deleted Footage
Moving from Prophetic Obliviousness
to Prophetic Consciousness

There's a need to move from prophetic obliviousness to prophetic conscious-ness. Obliviousness means lacking mindful attention, lacking active, conscious awareness. The discipline of awareness is key to prophetic evangelism; many open doors to share Christ can be missed by those who don't sense the opportuni-ties. It takes sensitivity to know the right approach. God wants us to have an eye-opening experience.

Recently I was given a spiritual picture of my head on the Father's chest (my ear over His heart), while my arm was extended and my fingers on the dial of a com-bination lock to a treasure safe. This symbolizes the need to be sensitive and inti-mate with the Father's heart, which in turn would give a prophetic evangelist the access code to the hearts of people, in order to release treasures out of darkness (Isaiah 45:3).

When you receive the power of the Spirit, you are attuned to the leading of the Lord in a new way. In Matthew 10:16, Jesus tells us to "be wise as serpents and innocent as doves." I've often struggled trying to get a handle on what Jesus meant. A serpent is a creature that is consciously focused and sensitive to its envi-ronment. A serpent has an extra-sensory organ in the roof of its mouth called "Jacobson's organ." This organ sharpens its sense of smell, allows for phenome-nal eyesight, and enables the detection of motion and vibrations. The serpent accomplishes this by constantly flicking out its tongue, by which it collects parti-cles. These particles of its immediate environment are brought into the serpent's mouth and dropped off in "Jacobson's organ." That's right; a serpent takes a con-stant reading of its surroundings.

Like a serpent, as soon as the heart and soul of a person are focused upon the spirit—your senses begin to receive that with which you're in contact with spiritually. In Luke 5:22, it says that "Jesus perceived their thoughts" and answered them accordingly. Jesus could deal with resistances and walls within people because of His consciousness; just think of how effective your witness could become! The secret of prophetic evangelistic consciousness eludes scientif-ic investigation, and the process of spiritual inspiration resists exact definition. In other words, don't try to figure it out—just flow with it!

In 2 Kings 6:17, Elisha prayed over his servant that God would "open his eyes that he may see." Elisha's servant moved from prophetic obliviousness to prophetic consciousness in one prayer. Begin that prayer over your life today and watch your spiritual vision become 20/20 for divine appointments.

Alternate Endings
Wet Sacrifices and The Elijah Anointing

You don't want to miss the W.A.T.T. that the Elijah anointing is not some exclusive and elusive mantle that only the two witnesses in Revelation will possess. It's important for you to realize that this anointing is reserved for you. The Elijah anointing has two components consisting of 1) a touch and 2) a timing. Malachi tells us that this anointing will pave the way before Jesus returns (a timing) and will redirect affections and hearts (a touch). You're in the right time and will walk in this life-altering, heart-rending touch for the task. Modern slang says, "you've got to get in where you fit in." **The Elijah anointing will open doors and give you full access and backstage passes to get behind enemy lines and connect to the hearts of a generation.**

"When we live in that place of consistency, we get to walk with God into the unpredictable and outrageous."
- Graham Cooke

Another W.A.T.T. is seen on Mt. Carmel (1 Kings 18:33-34) before Elijah called down fire on the cut bull. He had the sacrifice doused with water three times. This move seemed to be unusual on the backdrop of a water shortage (national drought). **This made the miracle more startling and compelling. The message for us is clear: God still sends fire on wet sacrifices.** Maybe you feel your efforts have been doused, your dreams have been dampened, or your life experiences have been moistened with your own tears. Disappointment can be overcome. Yet Elijah's miracle still speaks of the audacity of the God you serve, so don't be intimidated or shy away from the landing spot of His holy fire. Know that God desires to take underdogs to make them overcomers.

Reinhard Bonnke says, "Preaching salvation must be more than a cold water business. Conversions come in the fire." Many preachers don't mention the fact that Elijah's life was on the line; if fire had not fallen, his head would have rolled. Like Elijah, you must put your reputation, resources, and relationships on the line to connect people to God's lifeline.

Outtakes Countdown

10. Recapture some of the DNA of the past and sow it in the present to possess a different future. This principle is found in John the Baptist (Malachi 4:5-6, Matthew 11:14). God put Elijah's spiritual DNA in John, who became the historic forerunner for Jesus. Take time to find out what aspects of Elijah's DNA God wants to manifest through you.

9. You can never be trusted with prominence until you've learned to be content with obscurity. You can never be trusted with prominence until you've learned to be content with obscurity. You must see your ego sanctified and have ambition only for the King. This can happen only if you're willing to be hidden in Christ. It's not about your ministry, but His. John was content being in the wilderness and insisted, "I must decrease so Christ can increase."

8. True revival is not so much in what you portray, but in what you possess. It's not enough for you to put on something; God must put you on! In Judges 6:34, God put Gideon on and brought a nation to its knees. Where are the Gideons of our day?

7. Fight and recruit at the same time. In the national army, when you've been in for a while, you can become a recruiter. You must be a freedom fighter and enlist other people to fight for freedom.

6. Be convinced that you have a heart-turning anointing and ministry. If you don't acknowledge this dynamic unction, you won't activate it. John the Baptist preached against rulers, customs, and the predominant madness because he knew he had what Elijah had. You have this anointing, too!

5. Don't overlook the greatest miracle—the miracle within you. Christ in you is the hope of glory. You don't have to wait for something to fall from heaven to complete you; you already have what you need. You are a miracle. It's not enough to hear of one, we must become one.

4. Know that your emergencies become platforms for the Holy Spirit's emergence.
Nothing will attract a miracle like simple child-like dependence on God in the midst of the impossible. Everybody wants a miracle, but nobody wants to be put in a situation where they have to have one. Don't sweat it; God's got your back.

3. Know that only authentic, genuine light can cut through darkness. Become hell's worst nightmare—one genuine, bona fide believer. If you're for real, you'll see that God is for real, and so will the people you witness to.

2. Elijah had to "cut the bull" (1 Kings 18:33). The cut the bull principle says that you must do away with all shenanigans and showmanship and be about the Father's business. You must have an anointed and relevant witness. Pray for Christian television y'all!

1. Recognize that you can only echo the static around you if you never take time to escape it. Enough said!

Prophetic Evangelism – Field Activation Manual
Scene Study
Fill In the Blanks

Q. 1. The _____ of the anointing of Elijah is emphasized by the fact that it is called upon in the_____ situations.

Q. 2. What does the lifeless staff represent?

_____

_____

_____

_____

Q. 3. What was said about the Welsh revival and the fire of this movement?

_____

_____

_____

_____

Extensive Scene Study
Bonus Questions

Q. 1. How can we grow in the Elijah anointing?

_____

_____

_____

_____

Q. 2. How is Elijah's experience with the child who was dead an illustration of prophetic evangelism?

_____

_____

_____

_____

Q. 3. With whom did the Welsh revival begin?

_____

_____

_____

_____

Behind the Scenes
Discussion Questions

Discussion Location: Desert, forest, or park.

Discussion Experience: Set the stage by talking about Elijah and how God used him to do mighty exploits.

1. Name some fears, struggles, needs, and weak points that are present in the lives of an unsaved person or group of people in your life. Explain how being right with Christ would eliminate these personal problems.

2. How would the prophetic anointing help you in the area of evangelism?

3. Identify two of the eight exploits of Elijah that you would like to see in your life. Why?

4. Many Christians have the mentality noted in *Prophetic Evangelism*, "Get the lost into the church, and we'll get programs for them." Discuss how this mentality is contrary to the Bible, and discuss ways how we, as Christians, can "go into all the world."

5. *Prophetic Evangelism* states, "We will be convincing because we are convinced." Why are you convinced of Jesus Christ?

Cutting Room Floor
Application

"A prophetic evangelist can break things wide open; you can talk to someone who is hardened and God can give you a word for them."
– *Sean Smith*, Prophetic Evangelism

Video Survey Witnessing: In groups of two, find and talk to five people in any given area, such as a mall, college campus, or coffee shop. One person will be the interviewer, and one person will videotape the interview.

The object of this exercise is to pray that God will give you a word and an opportunity to speak in a way that God can use you to change a life. Before you leave, pray that God will give you the anointing of Elijah that will challenge, repair, loose, expose, and heal. Come up with five questions that you can ask people on the street that will open the door of opportunity and lead to a discussion of Christ.

The Making of an Epic
Journaling

1. Write about your Video Survey Witnessing experience.

2. Write briefly about the characteristics of Elijah that you long to have in your life.

3. Describe the steps that you are making to gain these characteristics.

Journal Notes

Journal Notes

Chapter 8

The Sons of Issachar - Soundwave Remix

"All great leaders have one characteristic in common; it is the willingness to confront unequivocally the major anxiety of their people in their time."
– *Author John Galbraith*

A lot of folks hide behind statements that are smokescreens. You have to listen for the voice of their hearts.

1 Corinthians 2:13
These things we also speak, not in words which man's wisdom teaches but which the Holy Spirit teaches, comparing spiritual things with spiritual.

> *A lot of folks* HIDE
> BEHIND *statements that*
> *are* SMOKESCREENS.
> *You have to listen for the*
> VOICE *of their hearts. .*

Favorite Scene Selections
Sons of Issachar

This is my favorite scene in this chapter because of my fascination with the legendary exploits of the sons of Issachar. They were so important to their culture, that David included them in his army—they were the CIA, CNN, and the 700 Club all in one.

In Acts 14:1, the Bible says that Paul and Barnabas "so spoke that a great multitude both of the Jews and of the Greeks believed." I've made it my life study to find out what it means to "so speak." What is it that would cause this witness to be followed by the diverse multitudes getting saved? What is created when you speak? Aristotle, speaking on the power of words said, "A man can confer the greatest of benefits by a right use of these and inflict the greatest of injuries by using them wrongly." You must become a student of effective communication.

The sons of Issachar also teach us that when it comes to evangelism, it is far better to become an in-the-moment learner than an expert planner. Adaptability is the master of skill; embrace it. You must become more skillful and practiced at helping people feel alive and connected to the gospel. By doing this, what you share will be more attractive and remembered. When you can present concepts and truth in nugget-sized packages, it can easily land on the person you're witnessing to, and that person can pass them on to others easily, too.

When witnessing, open up new worlds for people in their thinking, feelings, and priorities. Pull the rug out from under others, but quickly give them a new chair to fall into on their way down. Draw on a missing question or a tired assumption, challenge a strongly held belief, plant a seed of a different crop, or give them words to express what they feel but are barely able to describe. Relevance is a matter of position and focus. **You are relevant only when you relate to what the Holy Spirit is doing.** He is always relevant! We either get into the mainstream of revelation or fall into the swamp of business-as-usual church "politics."

Author Leonard Sweet is right when he says, "visual language (metaphor evangelism, metaphor preaching) is no longer 'an option.'" He goes on to say, "The ability to turn a metaphor will be key in the midst of our visual-holic generation." Like the man on the commercial says, "Can you hear me now?"

You must try to open up the eternal world for people in their mentalities and seek for the unchurched person's response. Page 131 in *Prophetic Evangelism* describes the need to interpret the inner yearning and the anguish of the culture. Only by staying alert to cultural movements and spiritual currents can we "so speak" to the conversion of diverse crowds. Ask yourself, "What's going on in society that's on the mind of the people I'm meeting with?"

Director's Bonus Commentary
Describe or Inscribe

This is a battle for the imagination of our generation. Jesus, with some phenomenal insight, answered some Pharisees who were looking to trap Him; it was definitely a word of wisdom. When asked in Matthew 22:15-22 if Jesus paid taxes to Caesar, Jesus responded by asking whose inscription was on the coin. The answer was, of course, Caesar's, but whose inscription can be placed upon the soul of humanity but God's alone? Jesus said give to Caesar what is Caesar's, but give unto God what is God's. All Caesar could put his image on was a coin, but God can put His image on you.

God's signature move is to leave an indelible impression upon human hearts. In Acts 17:23, while passing through Athens, Paul found an altar with an inscription "to the unknown god." Every unbeliever has this inscription upon his heart until God can use someone to rewrite the inscription and leave a divine invoice. Describe or inscribe? When we give facts about a phenomenon, we are describing it. **When God breathes upon our words, He is inscribing them upon the hearts and minds of our hearers.**

We've often given descriptions where an inscription was needed. I got saved, partially because I couldn't shake the words spoken to me by some college Christians at the University of the Pacific. The practical difference between descriptions and inscriptions is to articulate the mind of Christ combined with the presence of God to that individual. Today, seek to move from striving and describing to becoming effective at inscribing. As my friend Jeff Rostocil says, "Tattoo your world!" Selah!

Deleted Footage
Opening the Ears and Loosening the Tongue

The spirits that Jesus most often cast out in His time were an unclean spirit and a deaf and dumb spirit. In Mark 7:31-35, Jesus healed the speech impediment by loosening the tongue of the one brought to Him. Many Christians feel handicapped by a speech impediment that prevents them from speaking fluently and freely about their faith. The answer is found in God opening your ears to get you to speak correctly.

Speech impediments dissolve when hearing impairment is repaired. This is the essence of the awakened ear and the tongue of the learned. **We need to pray for a steady release of words of wisdom in our witnessing opportunities.** These prophetic smart bombs are crucial in the hard cases. Ask God in prayer to pour through you and give you the words to speak.

I've found that often God's Spirit refuses to compete with any other voices or distractions in our lives. He demands your full attention—if you can learn to stay tuned while on the fly, you will be more effective in the tongue of the learned.

I love it when God told Moses, "I will be with your mouth and teach you what you shall say" (Exodus 4:12). The shaded boxes on pages 140 and 141 in *Prophetic Evangelism* cast light on this subject. I also recommend studying the "Action Step Addendum" on "Tapping into God's Frequency."

Finally I want you to have assurance in these three areas: 1) God's grace will enable your "unables" to speak; 2) God's presence will accompany your words; and 3) you will have heaven's sound, which will resonate within others' hearts. I'm convinced that just as when you teach a kid to ride a bike and give her a soft spot to fall, so too does God allow us to have a soft spot to fall on as we leap into prophetic evangelism. As you lead others in prophetic evangelism, also give them some soft spots to land on to ease their initial experiences.

Alternate Endings
Soundwaves and Soundtracks

Every born-again Christian is called by the Lord to be a 24/7 witness. It's a gifting we should not neglect. **The first W.A.T.T. of this chapter is the realization that you must come with a fresh perspective.** Eighteenth-century evangelist George Whitefield attracted large crowds everywhere he went. He often preached open air because no hall could accommodate the crowd. His style of communication differed from most preachers in that day because he preached extemporaneously with a theatrical style. It made him the most popular preacher of colonial America.

Erasmus, a Reformer, was never at a loss for words; he was a master of a free-flowing style that was full of various fresh examples to illustrate any point. I believe that if you listen, you will hear echoes of the Reformation, and you will come with a fresh perspective as you become God's echo (John 12:49, John 8:38).

Aimee Semple McPherson founded the Foursquare denomination, and she released God's soundwave using the media and dramatized sermons. She was the grandmother of human videos and illustrated sermons. She had a tremendous following in Los Angeles and even Hollywood. She was fresh! **Bottom line, if you will follow God's soundwave and speak to the unmet needs and unfulfilled moments and avoid "Christianese," you will be a modern-day Reformer.** Don't be religious, just be yourself and remember that authenticity attracts.

George Barna says, "Until we present the message in ways that penetrate the consciousness of the people we seek to influence for Christ, we have not truly communicated. We have only made noise." There's a difference between religious noise and God's soundwave. The key is to speak the truth in love (Ephesians 4:15). We must be fresh, but we have got to make sure that we're serving up the truth; you can be fancy, but don't forsake the bread and butter, which is the gospel.

Finally, you must take God's soundwave and become God's authentic soundtrack to modern culture. You must hear God's prophetic message and become a prophetic message to your generation. On the day of Pentecost, a sound from heaven came and "it filled the whole house." I'm convinced that God is going to release a new soundwave (God's words of wisdom mixed with His presence from your lips) that will fill the whole body of Christ. Today begin to position yourself for laying this soundwave to your soundtrack by applying the following directions:

1.) **Meditate upon God's Word**
2.) **Spend time worshipping in God's presence**
3.) **Share God's Word actively in different ways**
4.) **Listen to great communicators of God's Word**
5.) **Track with the heart-felt expressions of the unsaved**

Outtakes Countdown

10. **Remember that words set the parameters of how people will react to you.** You must be fully aware of the words you use just as a doctor is conscious of the drugs he prescribes.

9. **Make question-asking an art.** You must realize that well-crafted questions are stealth bombs. Spend some time devising and praying over the questions you'll ask in prophetic evangelism scenarios.

8. **In witnessing, the bullets in your gun include:**
   a. Knowledge
   b. Clarity
   c. Control
   d. Humility
   e. Connectability

   You must fully implement each of these qualities in conversation and public sharing of your faith. Control is not be confused with controlling; it is having the self-control piece of the fruit of the Spirit. We've seen athletes attack the fans; we can't lose control like that and go after people in the stands of modern life.

7. **Practice responding without judgment in conversation.** Unsaved people immediately know if you're judging them. This polluted spring contaminates the spring of loving conviction seizing their hearts. Their only issue is what they are going to do with Jesus, so just preach Christ; don't play Holy Spirit to them.

6. **Look for the gift of a word of wisdom (1 Corinthians 12:8):**
   a. This is an inspired insight that becomes a key to unlocking a situation.
   b. This divine wisdom is given for the understanding of a problem and its solution. It is absolutely startling!
   c. This gift enables a person to speak both creatively and righteously concerning a tough circumstance or some drama.
   d. Wisdom enables you to avoid people's danger zones and allows you to speak constructively into a delicate situation.
   e. Words of wisdom usually come in the back-and-forth volley of conversation.

5. **Interview a variety of nonchurched people.** Become a treasure-hunter of cultural preferences (1 Corinthians 9:19-23) to become precise in your delivery of the message of hope. This way you can state the arguments that the person will receive first.

4. **If you can't defend your virtues and values, you'll fall prey to philosophies that aren't in your best interest.** You must be ready to give a defense for what you believe and be solid in that (1 Peter 3:15).

3. **Build an arsenal of redemptive analogies.** You should collect stories and illustrations that readily release the truth in understandable packages for the unsaved.

2. **Role play the scenario that you're interviewed on Oprah or preaching open-air.**
   Think of how you would relate the gospel to a nonchurched, postmodern-thinking individual. This practice will do wonders for accelerating your "tongue of the learned."

1. **Don't avoid sharing your faith for fear of offending.** It's better to offend than to never present the truth. Only the truth can set them free (John 8:32); opinions amuse, philosophies enslave, traditions can be binding, but truth always liberates.

Prophetic Evangelism – Field Activation Manual
Scene Study
Fill In the Blanks

Q. 1. What is evangelism defined as?

_____

_____

_____

_____

Q. 2. The sons of Issachar could look about and see into things and interpret the _____ written upon a_____.

Q. 3. What is a word of wisdom?

_____

_____

_____

_____

Q. 4. The major difference between _____and _____ is their ability to decode and deliver their culture.

Q. 5. What is *kerygma* defined as?

_____

_____

_____

_____

Q. 6. How do you have the tongue of the learned?
   a. Relate to people out of _____assumptions, not _____ assumptions.
   b. _____ people on _____ mutual ground.
   c. Be an active _____.
   d. Speak to the _____, _____needs, and _____ moments that drive people's lives.
   e. Fully utilize _____, _____, and redemptive _____.

Extensive Scene Study
Bonus Questions

Q. 1. What is the difference between new school apologetics and old school apologetics?

_____

_____

_____

_____

Q. 2. What is a fresh, redemptive way to phrase the gospel in only a paragraph?

_____

_____

_____

_____

Q. 3. The Hebrew word for _____ is also the word for _____.

Behind the Scenes
Discussion Questions

Discussion Location: Classroom

1. Which of your actions will people remember?
   a. Which ones will God remember?
   b. Which audience are you living to be remembered by?

2. The unsaved don't want to come to our churches, but they want to spend time with Jesus.
   a. Have you ever felt this way? Why?
   b. What can be done to change the appeal of the church?

3. What do you currently know about the following subjects?
   a. Political times
   b. Public affairs
   c. The temper of your nation
   d. The tendencies of present events

4. It is said that the sons of Issachar understood the times that they lived in. That statement has also been made about Master's Commission, Chi Alpha,

and many other ministries. Why is it important that we stand in that place?

5. Describe the gospel in a paragraph and present it to the group.

6. What words and phrases do you use that do not mean anything to the world, such as "let the river flow" or "start a fire in me"?

Cutting Room Floor
Application

The tongue of the learned and the awakened ear doesn't need a face. Pick a topic that you have interest and background in and research it on the Internet and in books. Go into an online chat room where that subject is being discussed and engage in conversation about that subject. If the moment opens itself to you, present the gospel in the chat room.

The Making of an Epic
Journaling

Doug Addison made this statement: "I am not ashamed of the gospel…but I am ashamed of how some Christians communicate it."

1. With the application in mind, journal what happened in the chat room and your thoughts about how Christians present the gospel.

2. In what ways can you help to change this perception?

Journal Notes

Journal Notes

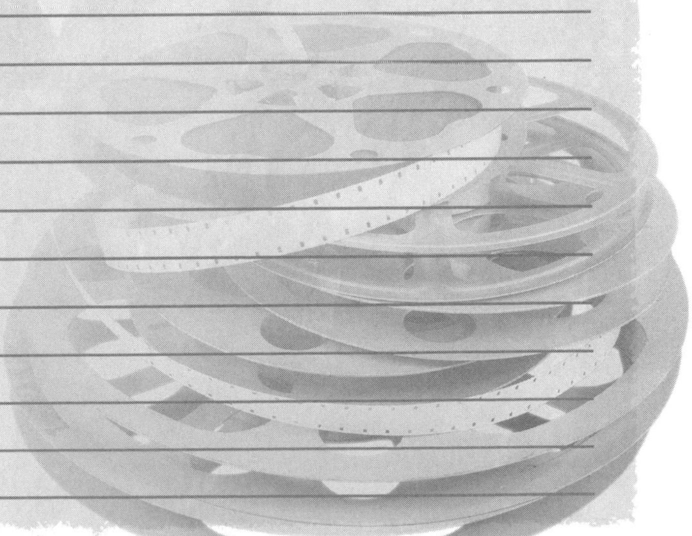

Chapter 9

Heaven's Paranormal Made Normal

"People increasingly long for the mystical and the spiritual rather than the evidential and facts-based faith of modern soil."
– *Dan Kimball*

"The Bible frequently points us toward experiences that we have not already had, implying that as we have these experiences we will grow in biblical knowledge."
– *John Wimber*

Favorite Scene Selections
Arrested Attention

My favorite section is "Arrested Attention." I can't emphasize enough how important it is to have something that can break through the trance-like spell our culture has on people's minds. I believe that God has great mysteries and miracles poised to be released into our generation. Within the postmodern shift comes a new openness to areas of Christian faith such as human spirituality, the existence of the supernatural, and a search for the transcendent. Many would not have believed Jesus without the supernatural element in His life. **You must present Christianity as a supernatural world to be explored, not as a rational puzzle to be solved.**

Romance and mystery lead the pack among best-selling books. The human heart is looking for someone to love and a mystery to solve. It's time to move away from an empty form of religion that seeks to comprehend God to a relationship that seeks to encounter God. **We don't operate from a place of mastery, but a place of mystery.** God has many ways of communicating—He can manifest His presence through miracles so we can experience Him.

Jesus never had a problem drawing a crowd (see Luke 6:17-19, 7:11, 8:19) and implementing the dinner bell of Christianity, which is the demonstration of the supernatural. Even when Jesus withdrew, the crowds sought Him (Luke 4:42). Jesus was a compassionate whirlwind of mystery. A mystery never lets you figure it out (Mark 6:2), but it never lets you go on to something else; a mystery forces an examination point in the spectator's heart.

Our world is fast accelerating into an age of supernatural awareness. Our desire to hear from the spirit has spawned a host of celebrity mediums and psychics for hire. People today are looking for truth that is experiential; the experience must now come before the explanation. Sometimes you have to shock and awe the mind supernaturally to arrest the heart of the spiritually challenged. The bottom line is that your success comes by the Spirit of the Lord.

Director's Bonus Commentary
Capitalizing on Your Mysteries

"Too often in the history of the Church, Christians have been apologetic for the mysteries of our faith, rather than capitalizing upon them."
– *Michael Sullivant*

Ephesians 6:19
...and for me, that utterance may be given to me, that I may open my mouth boldly to make known the mystery of the gospel...

A classic example of capitalizing on your mysteries is found on the day of Pentecost in Acts 2. In verses 2-6, it says that a "sound from heaven occurred and the multitude came together." Many Christians today would seek to downplay this event, yet Peter stood up, preached the gospel, and 3,000 people got saved. Many times I've seen people come to Christ after unusual dreams, demonic or angelic encounters, divine manifestations or signs and wonders. Peter followed up this harvest upon the heels of a miracle, with another in Acts 4:4. After seeing a lame man healed, Peter capitalized again on his mystery.

We see that darkness is capitalizing on its counterfeit mysteries and selling secularism or offering the occult behind its new age wares. We have shows on mediums talking to the dead, talk shows including psychic advisors, and pet psychic specialists on animal channels. You must be expectant and eager to send your message home after heaven's demonstrations. Moses' rod was meant to allow Moses to capitalize on its mystery in order to free Israel. Look for your rod's special effects (gifts of the Spirit) and seek to step out into God's miracles in public and your marketplace.

Finally, miracles make the demands of God seem not so unreasonable. **Here are five steps to help you capitalize on God's mysteries:**

1. **Don't analyze**—stay free from cranial roadblocks, which allow only logic-based information through.

2. **Be childlike**—children are always trusting of their daddy and will step into things without extra baggage.

3. **Respond quickly**—a lot of times God's open doors can be time-sensitive, and the law of diminishing returns applies to our faith and how instantaneous our obedience is.

4. **Embrace what God is doing**—if God is on the inside of something, what are you doing on the outside?

5. **.Let God be God**—sometimes we forget and try and be God jr. in situations where it's hard for us to relinquish control to God.

Deleted Footage
Having a Mystery Mindset

The presence of the supernatural really speeds things up. Unchurched people can bypass stages and steps of coming to faith when the presence of the supernatural bypasses the brain and goes directly to the heart.

Whenever a naturalistic mindset becomes dominant in an area, the release of the Holy Spirit's demonstrations becomes less prevalent. **To be too controlled is to be out of control—at least out of the Holy Spirit's control.** Religion idolizes concepts and avoids personal encounters with God. You mustn't make the mistake of valuing ideas and concepts above experiences with results.

> *Religion* IDOLIZES CONCEPTS *and avoids personal* ENCOUNTERS *with God.*

How do you define what is normal for an individual in whom lives the Spirit that raised Christ Jesus from the dead? Remember that John Wimber said, "The Bible frequently points us toward experiences that we have not already had, implying that as we have these experiences, we will grow in biblical knowledge." **A mystery mindset is a strong desire and determination to discover and practice all that Christianity was meant to be.**

Pastor Bill Johnson said it best when he said, "It is abnormal for a Christian not to have an appetite for the impossible. It has been written into our spiritual DNA to hunger for the impossibilities around us to bow at the name of Jesus." A powerless, demonstration-less Christian is an oxymoron.

Here's a startling discovery. In Matthew 22:29, Jesus told the Sadducees that one could be in error not only for being ignorant of truth, but also for not knowing the power of God. The original language reflects that one could be off by not experiencing the state of *"dunamis,"* which is the dynamite, explosive, miracle-working power. Bill Johnson also says, "The only way you consistently do kingdom works is to view reality from God's perspective."

In Mark 8:14-21, Jesus warned the disciples to "beware of the leaven of the Pharisees and Herod." He did this because they lost their miracle-mystery mindset and forgot Jesus' miracle of multiplying the five loaves to feed the five thousand. The leaven was a toxic mindset of skepticism and faithlessness. This mindset overrode the understanding of Christ's nature and the fragments phenomenon.

After every move of God, it's important to gather up the "fragments," which are the lasting evidences of God's move. The miracle of the multiplication took place in the hands of the disciples and they had the evidence to show people. God wants to release a miracle of multiplication in you to give you fragments to show people. These fragments are meant to spark faith for subsequent miracles and yield a miracle-mystery mindset, which means that God has thought patterns for you to follow.

"Jesus had a supernatural conception, a supernatural ministry, a supernatural sacrifice, and a supernatural resurrection. He started the church with a supernatural experience: supernatural fire and wind and caused them to speak with supernatural tongues. He caused supernatural signs and wonders to be by the hands of the church. God confirmed his word spoken by the church members with supernatural healings and miracles. The supernatural should be expected, not unexpected; the normal, not the abnormal!"
– *Pastor Frank Damazio*

One final thought. Some leaders and Christians are uncomfortable with the supernatural dimension when non-Christians are giving audience to it. My feeling is that if you allow people to track with you, they will go along for the ride. Here's an example: if I were to walk up to you and throw a Gatorade chest of fishy water all over you, you would be ticked like the Hulk, but when you come to Sea World, pass into the splash zone seating, and Shamu splashes down, something similar happens. At that point, whale bath water hits you leaving you soaked, and you're all right with that. No fits, no fussing, no fights! Why? Because to be forewarned is to be forearmed. You need to go with the supernatural and tell the bystanders, "you will get wet!"

Alternate Endings
Go with the Force

The first W.A.T.T. in this chapter is the importance of turning aside to investigate when you witness God's mystery manifestations. These mystery manifestations are when God releases signs or the aspects of His nature that are supernatural. After Jesus led Peter to his historic and massive fish catch (Luke5:5-9), all who were there "were astonished at the catch of fish."

The original Greek reveals that they were "taken possession of," "seized," and "left in wonder." This is why a mystery manifestation is so important and crucial to unlocking the harvest. You must take time to investigate things at your marketplace post, campus, and neighborhood. Look and expect God's movement to jump-start your movement and engage you in witnessing opportunities. Unexplainable shifts in life cause openness in the hearts of seekers. I believe that God is going to make guest appearances in the lives of unbelievers a lot more commonplace. Some of you have got to do like Luke Skywalker and put down the manual, which equates to our programs and intellectual approaches, and go with the Force, God's supernatural way!

Leave this lesson with a new world view, one that embraces the trans-rational aspect of God's personality. We don't realize how much the enemy has used a secular western world view (your grid for how you view life) to undermine an understanding of true biblical Christianity. God wants you to have a supernatural, eternal kingdom world view that releases a miraculous life, instead of resisting it.

If the idea of you ministering in signs and wonders sounds too "out there," you need to discover the worldview of Jesus. Your set of assumptions about the world around you controls your thinking. Don't be ashamed to testify about miracles and answers to prayers. Don't disbelieve divine intervention in any situation. **Don't be intimidated to confront any need, problem, or demon for the gospel's sake.** Finally, don't hesitate to pray about anything; you may have a testimony in the making.

Don't let this fact escape you: you must become dissatisfied with where you are to get where you need to be. Author Leonard Sweet says, "Western Christianity went to sleep in a modern world governed by the gods of reason and observation. It is awakening to a postmodern world open to revelation and hungry for experience." **Remember, the benefit of flowing with God's mysteries is that He witnesses of Himself better than you do.** You don't have to defend a lion; you just have to let it out of its cage.

Outtakes Countdown

10. Embrace the mystery. Learn to live a life in the Spirit, where you don't have to have it all figured out. Be willing to endure uncertainty. Revisit God's original IMAX experience (Exodus 20:18-21) and visualize what it must have looked like, smelled like, sounded like, and felt like.

9. God is not your copilot; He must be your sole pilot. Give the Holy Spirit more space and opportunities to direct you in decisions and situations. It's about you relinquishing control in exchange for a God-directed flight (Proverbs 3:5-6).

8. Recognize that God is after transformations, not just transactions. God is not just about getting information to you, but giving the "e-factor," a life-altering experience with Him.

7. Personal purity prepares one to witness God's wonders (Joshua 3:5). Seek to be cleansed consistently from the defilement of everyday life. Consecrate your mind, will, emotions, and body to the Lord afresh to be used by Him. When God sees you show up, you will see God show off.

6. Today, allow God to redefine what "normal" Christianity means. Additionally, allow the Holy Spirit to make new entries in that "living" definition within your life. Mysteries of God are waiting to be manifested in a vessel in this hour. Are you the one, or should we look for another?

5. Take it to the bone (Ezekiel 37). In the valley of dry bones, Ezekiel didn't try to trivialize the dilemma; he left it in God's hands and obeyed. Yet, he realized the solution and the means to dispense the remedy called for him to "take it to the bone." You must possess this flexibility, while maintaining urgent focus. Take it to heart and go the distance.

4. Pray for an increase in the gift of discernment of spirits.
a. This gift is trans-rational; it's beyond Spiderman's tingling spider sense.
b. This gift allows you to examine and evaluate a phenomenon, manifested mystery, and prove what God's will is in it.
c. This gift has a deep underlying spirit of conviction that does not allow you to rest when you know people have been given a half-truth or false teaching.
d. This gift allows you to know what spirit is behind people's actions and lives.

3. **Quest to manifest (Ephesians 5:13, Colossians 4:4, 1 John 3:10).**
   Meditate on these passages, memorize them, and allow God to grow a desire
   to make visible what has been previously invisible.

   Manifest defined—"to make visible and known what has been hidden or
   unknown, whether by words or deeds."

2. **Ask God to allow you to hear the inaudible and see the invisible.** The
   backdrop of the spirit realm affects all that you witness in your natural
   world. This also affects your effectiveness in witnessing.

1. **Shorten the commute between dreaming of your next experience with
   God and being in one.** You must position yourself to get a backstage pass,
   behind the veil of God's manifest presence.

Prophetic Evangeilism - Field Activation Manual
Scene Study
Fill In the Blanks

Q. 1. The questions and debates cease when they see the _____ of God.

Q. 2. To manifest the mystery is to make _____what has been _____ and hidden, whether by _____ or _____, that which will _____ the mouth.

Q. 3. What is the most often mistaken phrase that people think is in the Bible?
_____
_____
_____
_____

Q. 4. What are the three enemies to letting the supernatural flow?
a. Failing to deal with our inner _____ _____.
b. The feeding frenzy of _____ acceptance and the secular _____.
c. Fear of the _____ or that which you can't _____.

Q. 5. What does the mystery accomplish?
a. It creates an awe of God that crushes _____.
b. The mystery of God sucks _____ right out of the atmosphere.
c. The mystery establishes a _____.
d. It causes a powerful _____of divine presence.
e. It _____ the deep cry of the human heart.

Extensive Scene Study
Bonus Questions

Q. 1. You have been _____to be touched by that which is _____.

Q. 2. When and why did Gnosticism begin to leap into the church?
_____
_____
_____
_____

Q. 3. What was the burning bush a picture of?

_____

_____

_____

_____

Q. 4. A _____ _____ is a modern _____ experience that the church in some areas fails to provide.

Behind the Scenes
Discussion Questions

Discussion Location: Look for an environment of wonder and mystery such as a cave, the Grand Canyon, ocean, or a mysterious wondrous place, or somewhere with an incredible unique history.

"If you don't understand the importance of mystery, you will be limited in being a prophetic evangelist because things will always have to make sense to you."
– *Sean Smith*, Prophetic Evangelism

1. Has God ever asked you to do anything that doesn't make sense to you?

"If we start to discount that which we find strange as being unbiblical, we soon find out that we wouldn't have very many pages left in the Bible."
– *Sean Smith*, Prophetic Evangelism

2. Of all the stories in the Bible, talk about one that when you first heard it you said, "Now that's strange."

3. The burning bush mentality described in *Prophetic Evangelism* speaks of a "fuel-less" fire, which means a fire that did not consume the bush. In other words, the bush was not the fuel. Where was the fuel? It was God. Have you ever experienced a time when supernatural strength empowered you to do something that you were unprepared do? Talk about this "fuel-less" fire experience.

"Satan doesn't have anything that's creative. All his powers are destructive, but God's given us the prophetic that is creative."
– *Sean Smith*, **Prophetic Evangelism**

4. What are some of the creative tools and ideas things you use in evangelism? Describe a time when you were speaking and you had no idea what you were saying, but God was speaking through you.

5. The three enemies of allowing the supernatural to flow are a) wanting to be in control, b) wanting to be accepted, and c) fear of the unknown. Which one of these is your greatest enemy?

Cutting Room Floor
Application

Word Devour: Choose 10 to 20 scriptures that speak of a mystery or a strange event. Use this with what we call Word Devour. Following are the steps to devouring the word prophetically.

1. Read verses from at least three versions of the Bible such as NIV, NKJ, NAS, or The Message.
2. Pick out at least two key words from each verse of the Bible.
3. Look up definitions of each key word and write them out.
4. Rewrite the scripture using the definitions instead of the next words. This will help you to gain better understanding of the text.
5. Read the passage from a commentary, like *Matthew Henry's Commentary*.
6. Write comments about what you read.
7. With your new understanding of the text, memorize it.
8. Using the passage, write out a sermon and prepare to present it. The sermon needs to have at least two illustrations and two quotes, and it must be 15 minutes long.
9. Present the sermon to one person in a conversation or in front of a group.

The Making of an Epic
Journaling

1. Have you ever felt like the young man who asked, "Would you pray for me, because my mind won't let my heart go free?" (*Prophetic Evangelism*). Write a prayer asking for freedom in your mind and for trust in God when you don't understand.

2. What mindsets hinder your heart from being free?

Journal Notes

Journal Notes

Chapter 10

Wanted: Miracle Workers In The Marketplace

"These are days of swift acceleration. Things are speeding up. Heaven is shouting: No hesitation."
– *Bobby Conners*

I believe that 90 percent of the devil's strategy is to keep you from stepping out, and 90 percent of the damage hell will feel is when you actually do step out.

Favorite Scene Selections Imposter Alert and the Consequences of a Dunamis Default

My favorite sections in this chapter are tied between "Imposter Alert" and "Consequences of a *Dunamis* Default." Recently a new crime of personal invasion has arisen that has even commercials making light of it. A commercial shows an elderly lady sitting in a lawn chair in the midst of a trailer park. She surprisingly begins to speak in a husky man's voice. The commercial warns you to protect yourself from identity theft. Identity theft is when someone takes on your personal identity traits to indulge in your benefits of access.

Recently I witnessed a Faith Week where students on a panel representing various beliefs fielded questions. The panel consisted of students from the National Paganistic Student Association, the Wiccan Student Association, and a historically religious organization that will remain nameless! After the first two representatives shared, it was obvious that they had vision, were inclusive, were growing, and possessed power to make a difference.

When the student representing the historical religion shared, he talked of having fun, having a survivor mentality, spiritual maintenance, and the human founder of his faith rather than the eternal founder of the church, Jesus Christ. Immediately, I felt the Holy Spirit speak the phrase "identity theft." The non-Christian counterfeits were saying what the "believer" *should* have been saying, and the "believer" was saying what should have been coming out of the nonbelievers' mouths.

You can't allow darkness to steal your proclamations and your practices. Darkness typically comes to flood the market with the counterfeit, sensing that

God is releasing the genuine. **Imposters can hold the mike only until the authentic takes the stage.** Satan's only chance is if you do not step up and step out in harvest opportunities. Let's take the devil's stick and beat him with it!

It's going to take some level of aggressiveness to enter into the unexplainable dimensions of what God has for you. I believe that you may be at a crossroads time in your life, wondering how to get from point A to point B, questioning how you'll rise above the mountains before you. The answer is in your relationship with the Holy Spirit and activating what He has already deposited inside of you. Allow Jesus to rise up and live big within you.

> *It's going to take some level of* AGGRESSIVENESS *to enter into the unexplainable dimensions of what* GOD HAS FOR YOU.

When I wrote "Consequences of a *Dunamis* Default," my thought process involved how much is at stake in this hour and the platform that you've inherited. The History Channel is filled with programs that ask "what if?" What if a pack of farmers doesn't resist "taxation without representation" in the American Revolutionary War? What if Rosa Parks gives up her rightful seat on a Montgomery bus? What if you and I remain silent and anonymous before the ultimate, cosmic destroyer of souls? You've got to face your dangers to complete your destiny.

Default means 1) loss due to not showing up, and 2) an option that is selected automatically unless an alternative is specified. A *dunamis* default says that if you and I don't enter into the tangible expression of God's deposit of power, we concede souls and cities. Darkness is then perceived as having the only supernatural prowess in the day that people live.

1 John 3:8 emphatically yet simply states that, "For this purpose the Son of God was manifested, that He might destroy the works of the devil." The word manifest, in the original, means "to make visible what has been hidden" or "to show one's self." The only way the works of the devil are destroyed is if Christ is manifested. The opposite of "destroy" is "to construct, build up, or flourish." Places where you and I hide, such as behind church walls, are in the same communities where witchcraft, perversion, and deception will be built up and flourish. **Your presence has been requested at the demolition of the darkness party taking place at a marketplace near you.** Who knows? This may be the day that the madness stops and history is made. You must know that you are empowered to be where you stand.

Director's Bonus Commentary
The Design of the Dunamis

Wherever a purpose is forgotten, abuse is inevitable. God is a God of purpose, and everything God creates is a solution to a problem. God's products are always redemptive. You've got a car to solve your transportation problem, you have the Internet to solve an information problem, and God made you to solve a humanity problem. Power tools have all but retired many labor-oriented old-school tools. The reason is that power gets the job done without wearing out the "handler" of the task and overcomes higher levels of resistance. You've got to have the power!

Jesus told the disciples in Acts 1:8, "You shall receive power...and you shall be witnesses to Me...to the ends of the earth." You weren't given power just to keep from being dysfunctional and to stay off some of the daytime talk shows. You were given power to become witnesses of the unseen kingdom of God.

Ephesians 3:20 tell us that God is able to do exceedingly, abundantly above all that we ask or think, according to the power that works in us. No matter how daunting your situation may appear to be, you have a power dwelling inside of you Who is ready to go to work. The devil can't stop God from operating within you, but you and I can disable the *dunamis* power from functioning in our lives.

Dunamis is a Greek word meaning strength, power, ability, and miracle-working facilitation and the power and influence of the mighty. Another major truth is that the Holy Spirit is a witnessing spirit (John 15:26-27). The Holy Spirit keeps reaching out to bring the reality and report of heaven to earth.

The purpose for the power is to get you in the ministry that keeps the Holy Spirit moving. This ministry is to win people to Christ and to disciple the nations of the world. The design of *dunamis* is not to keep your witness confined to a building, but to empower you as a missionary in the marketplace.

Author Robert Heidler notes, "The empowering of the Holy Spirit is the ministry by which the Spirit of God comes upon you with power to equip you for supernatural ministry." Once the Holy Spirit fell on Saul of Kish in 1 Samuel 10:6-7, Saul a) prophesied, b) was turned into another man, and c) could do as the occasion demanded. These are and always will be the reasons you receive power.

Deleted Footage
The Acts Advantage of Prophetic Evangelism

We have the book of Acts because the apostles acted; they didn't call it the book of "Intentions." Your spiritual forefathers weren't sitting cross-legged in some remote pasture contemplating how good it was in the upper room. This may seem like overkill, but this principle has become underrated in our time. You have to do something to know something. If you wait to know something before you do something, likely neither will happen.

The goal of every spirit, power, or intent is for ultimate expression in the realm of time and space. The invisible reality of the soul seeks to express itself through visible manifestations. The bottom line is that it's time to manifest; it's time to act and move upon what you know. We need to communicate the truth to somebody, instead of just thinking about it. When the truth leaves your lips, you have done something about it—you've put it into play. Movements in history—whether sociological, political, or spiritual—occurred because somebody went first; someone acted upon what they knew and possessed.

> MOVEMENTS IN HISTORY—*whether sociological, political, or spiritual—occurred because* SOMEBODY WENT FIRST; *someone acted upon what they knew and possessed.*

Following are the Acts advantages of prophetic evangelism:

1. Prophetic evangelism attracts an atmosphere of the sense of the nearness of God.

2. Prophetic evangelism forges a strong laser of inward convincing, which is undeniably heart-felt (1 Corinthians 14:24-25). This yields inward transformation that can pass intellectual defenses. There are two types of testimonies: internal and external. The internal testimony is the witness of the Holy Spirit within, and the external testimony is your consciousness of God's presence manifested.

3. Prophetic evangelism gives battle plans and battle supplies for the battle for souls (1 Timothy 1:18).

4. Prophetic evangelism yields holy audacity and *conation*. My friend Mario

Murillo defines conation as "the energy of the mind that produces an effort and an explosive desire to act on the voice of God." You act differently when you have insider information.

5. Prophetic evangelism allows a disciple to flow in the *kairos* (divine timing) moments with effectiveness (Acts 13:2-4). The lethal combo of prophetic giftings with an evangelistic gift not only called out Saul and Barnabas, but also called them to a hot spot ripe for change.

6. Prophetic evangelism becomes fuel and turbo-boosts our spiritual lives.
God is rising up an army of believers who are hungry to be used in their gifts, to strike at the present darkness, and to set people free. This chapter was intended to allow you to see what an impact Spirit-filled believers can have and what great exploits God will entrust them with. Their outcomes were either riots or revivals, but indifference was not on the menu. The early church was abandoned, not apathetic, and sought the power of God to fully accomplish His work. Begin to examine your life today and see if you possess any beliefs that fail to have accompanying action.

Once you experience the profound love that the Father wants to lavish on you, you will become an *agape* addict. Once you taste and see what prophetic evangelism is like, you will get hooked and want more. In the early church, understanding was experiencing. **Don't be prematurely satisfied with the acquisition of facts instead of experience.**

A major practical key to being released in a new "flow" is to hook up with a more experienced vessel. We learn best by having it modeled. Prophetic evangelism can be better facilitated if we step out two-by-two (like Jesus sent the disciples), asking the Holy Spirit to give you something for people. When you first learn to parachute, you do it in tandem, which helps you get over the fear. We need some tandem prophetic evangelism, so we can benefit from the experience of another.

Do something today! Be willing to take risks, start swinging for the fence. Use what you've got! Remember, the spirit of fear is a wimpy, *soufflé*, "pooh-butt" demon (an inner-city term for being weak and overmatched). So activate, instigate, communicate, and emulate the Master's ministry.

131

Alternate Endings
God's Extension Cords

The first walk-away timeless truth (W.A.T.T.) of this chapter is that you already possess what you need to get it done. The book of Acts church was equipped with the baptism, anointing, and gifts of the Holy Spirit to witness supernaturally to its generation, revealing the reality of Jesus's resurrection. Without the Holy Spirit, there would be no witness; there would be no success without His influence.

You are God's extension cord, plugged into heaven's outlet and available for needy appliances. God wants the issues of capacity and competence settled forever (Acts 1:8). You have no need to wait for something to fall from heaven; you have Jesus waiting on you to fall upon the needs around you.

The second W.A.T.T. of this chapter is the concept of conation. I learned this valuable revelation from evangelist Mario Murillo. Conation is a term in psychology that is described as the energy of the mind that brings forth effort. Conation, as Mario Murillo defines it, is:
a. **An explosive desire to act on the voice of God.**
b. **The inability to hesitate.**
c. **A violent God-given drive to succeed in the pursuit of a divine goal.**

In essence, conation says, "you'll have to kill me to stop me!" This chapter has the word "activated" in its title on purpose. All dealings of God become action. The Spirit of God will get you involved somewhere. It's one thing to own a net; it's another thing to cast it! Remember, God will not lead you into a situation where He will not "have your back."

The purposes of gifts are:
1. To demonstrate in a tangible way the compassion, attributes, and nature of God.
2. To destroy the works of darkness; this sets people free.
3. To evangelize the nations of the world, confirming our message.
4. To build up and encourage God's army.
5. To mirror the ministry of Christ and to guarantee the success of our mission.

Here's a bonus W.A.T.T. from this chapter. I want to give you some keys to releasing the prophetic gift in your life:
1. Prioritize intimacy over blessings.
2. Desire to flow in the prophetic (1 Corinthians 14:1).

3. **Be sensitive and go with the promptings and anointing "on the fly" in the marketplace.**

4. **Be led by love and be filled with the Holy Spirit (1 Corinthians 14:1).**

5. **Be bold and reject all fears**.

Outtakes Countdown

10. **Relinquish the right that you could ever have a belief that you don't act upon (James 2:17).** Modern Christianity has a lot of creeds, but we need to turn our creeds into deeds.

9. **Don't shrink back from the victory that lies ahead.** You must practice rising up in every situation to fulfill your high calling. Be willing to fail in order to prevail.

8. **Seek God for a fresh infilling of the Holy Spirit and for heaven's saturation, plain and simple.**

7. **Go ahead and dream with God.** Put a deadline on it! Don't let God's dream fade into a fantasy unimplemented. Many people receive a blueprint from heaven and spend their lives reveling in the diagrams and plans. No one settles for the blueprints alone; a structure or building must follow with an estimated completion date. A dream you don't pursue becomes a nightmare that haunts you.

6. **Place a demand on the anointing on your life.** Christians in the early church believed that when they prayed, the Spirit would show up accompanied by powerful manifestation. Step into the vacuum that summons the touch of God on your life to rise up.

5. **Find a friend, coach, or mentor to support you in these areas.** God ordains a "blacksmith" effect of a weapon-forming dynamic that occurs when we get sharpened by the anointing on others' lives (Proverbs 27:17).

4. **Move from a survival stage, past the blessing stage, to a proactive witness and prophetic evangelistic stage.** You've got to grow up to go up to the mark to which God has ordained for you. Many believers get stuck in the early stages, but you must keep moving on.

3. **Acknowledge that God wants to witness that He's in you more than you want to witness that you're in Him.** You must remember that releasing the mystery of the gospel is His idea. It took God to reveal God to people; it is a supernatural thing.

2. **Sign up to be a Holy Ghost activist (Hosea 12:9, Isaiah 44:8-9).** Your enemy has activated his witness; God has some Holy Ghost activators as well. Your prophetic witness will grow in the earth; it is ordained!

1. **Never fail to give God credit for the miracles and exploits (Zechariah 4:6).** You mustn't be fooled into thinking that it is because of you that people are touched and transformed (Acts 3:12).

Prophetic Evangelism - Field Activation Manual
Scene Study
Fill In the Blanks

Q. 1. I'm convinced that God still wants to speak directly into the lives of the lost through _____ _____.

Q. 2. When did Peter's doormat leadership capacity become totally and completely activated?

_____

_____

_____

_____

Q. 3. How are you forfeiting *dunamis* power in your city?

_____

_____

_____

_____

Q. 4. Why do you believe that Samaria went from awakening to bewitched?

_____

_____

_____

_____

Q. 5. What does the spirit of divination want to do to our generation?

_____

_____

_____

_____

Q. 6. What is the Peter factor?

_____

_____

_____

_____

Q. 7. What is the Philip factor?

_____

_____

_____

_____

Q. 8. What is the Paul factor?

_____

_____

_____

_____

Extensive Scene Study
Bonus Questions

Q. 1. What are some of the consequences of a *dunamis* default?

_____

_____

_____

_____

Q. 2. In the original text, what does the word "divination" mean?

_____

_____

_____

_____

Q. 3. Give a biblical example of how God used a dream or vision to speak to someone (do not include the stories mentioned in this book).

_____

_____

_____

_____

Behind the Scenes
Discussion Questions

1. What do you think revivalist John G. Lake meant when he said, "The life of the Christian, without the indwelling power of the Spirit in the heart, is weariness to the flesh?"

2. "Jesus can only be what you preach him to be."
   – *Sean Smith*, Prophetic Evangelism
   What have you preached Jesus to be?
   a. Is He more than that?
   b. What else is He?

3. "All it takes for evil to advance is for good men to do nothing."
   – *Sean Smith*, Prophetic Evangelism

   What evils are advancing in our world today? What can you do about it?

4. In the scriptures, prophetic dreams, visions, pictures, impressions, and enigmas have moved people from a place of unbelief to a place of faith. Has this ever happened to you or someone you know?

5. How is it possible for a mighty move of God to be followed by amazing deception?

6. If you're living in the will of God, what may seem to be a setback may actually be a divine setup. Have you ever experienced a divine setup that you thought was a setback in the beginning? Are you currently experiencing something that just might be a divine setup?

The Making of an Epic
Journaling

1. Has God ever given you a spiritual dream or vision? If so, write how it affected you or prepared you for what was to come. If not, ask God to give you a spiritual dream or vision.

2. Write a prayer asking for the sensitivity of the Spirit.

Journal Notes

_____
_____
_____
_____
_____
_____
_____
_____
_____
_____
_____
_____
_____
_____
_____
_____
_____
_____
_____
_____
_____
_____
_____
_____
_____
_____
_____
_____
_____
_____
_____

Journal Notes

Chapter 11

A Blueprint 4 An Exousia Mindset

"I can't hear what you are saying for what you are."
– *Atheist Bertrand Russell*

Favorite Scene Selections
Operating from Heaven's Vantage Point

I don't believe there is a person reading these truths who is not involved in a very deep struggle to rise to higher spiritual heights in order to be used of God.

There is a reason why "Operating from Heaven's Vantage Point" jumps out at me. It's because of the impact this truth has had on me. Having grown up in some challenging situations, I often struggled with the three big I's: 1) Inferiority 2) Inadequacy, and 3) Insecurity. I've had to meditate on these principles to rise above these grounding, opposing influences. **The Bible never gives the cosmetic touch-ups to hide the morning face of the biblical people that God would turn into giants of the faith.**

2 Peter 1:3-4 reminds you that you are divinely furnished for everything that life can throw at you, and that His promises are given to make you a partaker of the divine nature. What you must walk away with is that God never calls you to something that He doesn't authorize you to function in. The Angel of the Lord told Gideon in Judges 6:14, "Go in this might of yours, and you shall save Israel from the hand of the Midianites. Have I not sent you?" In other words, your enablement is built into your mandate; you are anointed inside and out.

This anointing within deals with *exousia; exousia* is God's delegated authority and power. God has given believers tremendous authority. **T.L. Osborn said, "Wherever I go, God always arrives on the scene." That's not arrogance; that's the necessary confidence for success in your mission.** Jesus has passed the baton and the Hebrew 11 faith hall-of-famers have passed the baton, and they are all waiting for you to bring it home.

This chapter is really about identity and identification. You have a new identity carved out of the Rock of Ages, and your identification must be with the One who possess all power. When sickness, sin, and Satan look at you, they must see the One who has the keys! When the opposition sees the One in you who has increased, they must decrease and deteriorate. Let God arise, and let the enemy be scattered (Psalm 68:1)!

Director's Bonus Commentary
What to Do When Your Authority Is Challenged

Many of us have had experiences where we've stepped out in an adverse circumstance representing God, only to walk away feeling less than successful. The first time I was involved in exorcising darkness out of a girl, this demonic voice told me that it wasn't going anywhere. After several hours it left, and after all of that I realized that it was only the peon spirit of fear. I later asked God, "Why did it take so long?" He responded, "Because the demon saw more of you than it did of Me." Ouch!

That experience set me in a direction that I have profited from to this day. The one thing that I did right was that I never gave up. When your authority is challenged, make sure you stay true to the task, never abdicating the authority the Lord has given you. Remind yourself and the resistive force of whose Name you represent and His *exousia* in that situation. Jesus once asked Peter, "Where is your faith?" when Peter failed to rebuke the storm. We also must be moved by faith and recognize where our faith is and should be rooted.

What you do when your authority is challenged is everything. True authority is reflected and proven when opposed; it doesn't fade, but flourishes. 2 Timothy 3:8-9 recalls how Moses' authority was challenged by the Egyptian magicians, Jannes and Jambres, but Moses outlasted the opposition. The most encouraging note is scripture's promise that the "opposition will progress no further" and their "folly will be manifest to all." If you don't let up, darkness will be forced to let go.

Deleted Footage
Spiritual Superconductivity

In science there is a law that governs the flow of electricity called the Theory of Superconductivity. This theory provided such a breakthrough in understanding that the first scientist who cracked the theory won the Nobel Prize.

Superconductivity is a phenomenon displayed by certain conductors (materials) that demonstrate no resistance to the flow of an electrical current. This happens without a loss of energy, and a superconductor can also produce powerful magnetic fields. A semiconductor behaves somewhat as an insulator (meaning that it offers resistance); it can conduct electricity at room temperature. If 100 volts were connected to one end of a superconductor, 100 volts would flow out of the other end due to its lack of resistance.

The anointing and authority within you is like electricity running through you. **Breaking it down and making it plain, a superconductor maximizes the flow of power, while a semiconductor has a power constipation problem that minimizes the flow.** Jesus said in Matthew 28:18-20 that "all authority has been given to Me in heaven and on earth" and went on to commission believers to make disciples of all nations. In Luke 10:19, Jesus said, "I give you the authority to trample on serpents and scorpions and over all the power of the enemy."

Putting it all together, the measure of authority that we're connected to is greater than what flows out of us. God wants to make you more of a superconductor and less of a semiconductor. What are the resistive issues in your life? What hinders the flow from issuing forth in abundance through you? Superconductivity allows electrical current to travel great distances with just a small amount of power lost to resistance. A kind of personal superconductivity will happen in your life as you walk with a revelation of authority and holiness.

A semiconductor Christian needs room temperature to flow right. A superconductor Christian can flow in a more hostile environment. A superconductor Christian produces a magnetic field. We, as prophetic evangelists, must use our gift of attraction to draw the lost and the presence of God. The attraction gift is the favor God puts in people's hearts when you're before them that causes them to be drawn to you. Repeat after me, "I'm attractive." Say it again!

> *A* SEMICONDUCTOR *Christian needs room temperature to flow right.* *A* SUPERCONDUCTOR CHRISTIAN *can flow in a more hostile environment.*

A semiconductor can increase in its conductivity, modeling that God wants to bring increase to your "flow." You've got more available in your spirit and in the heavenlies than you are currently apprehending. Decide today that you will be a superconductor, maximizing what God has placed inside of you, and dedicate yourself to God's process to produce it.

In Matthew 10:7-8, Jesus told His followers to share the kingdom message and flow in the supernatural, and He reminded them that "freely you have received, freely give." God has ordained a free flow of His essence through your life as you share the kingdom. Peter, in Acts 3, saw healing virtue flow through him to put a lame man on his feet and said to him, "such as I have, I give unto you." What Peter had could get through him unobstructed to reach others. Peter moved from a semiconductor to a superconductor, setting the early world ablaze.

It is not necessarily about getting more anointing in you, but allowing the anointing to flow through you. Out of the total flow of life that God wants to pass through you, how much actually makes it through? How much gets stopped up by some blockage?

Alternate Endings
Getting Your Ears Pierced

The first W.A.T.T. of this chapter is spiritual ear-piercing (Psalm 40:6-9). In ancient Israel a slave got pierced, which represents total loyalty and submission to one's master. They got pierced if they chose to remain in the service of their master after the obligatory six years. Spiritual ear-piercing allows you to flow in the authority of your Master. To the extent that your life is truly submitted to God, He will release you in His name.

True spiritual authority is the authority of a life; it's an authority that grows out of life and finds its flow in the life of the person holding the authority. Submission is not the denial of any gifting (false humility), but seeing yourself properly related to Christ. You must have that proper confidence of who you are in Christ and what you are with respect to God's calling on your life. In addition to submission, commitment accentuates or takes you to the next level in your authority. Nothing is as profound as the power of a committed life.

You have the challenge by Jesus's life to bring the reality of the kingdom into the lives of those around you. You are called to continue what began in Jesus and what was portrayed in the early church.

Here are four pointers to take from the Savior's ministry:
a. Jesus operated by the Spirit; He didn't operate independent of His Father.
b. Jesus directed His ministry to the oppressed and needy (Matthew 11:5). The works of Jesus were constantly directed to the poor.
c. Jesus confronted and challenged the authority of Satan. Satan may be the strongman, but Jesus is One who is stronger.
d. Jesus' movement was always redemptive. He sought to go to the root of the problem and He made a beeline for the real need.

The final **W.A.T.T.** comprises some quick tips for stepping into prophetic evangelism ministry opportunities:

1. **Activate your spirit**—you must remain accessible to the Holy Spirit, consistently paying attention to whatever God may be releasing to your spirit. Learn to walk and chew bubblegum at the same time, paying attention to the person and exercising your spirit simultaneously.

2. **See the invisible as well as the visible**—you must be alert to what you pick up visually while witnessing. Sometimes how a person looks can tell you something, yet ask God to show also you what's behind the scenes.

3. **Hear the inaudible as well as the audible**—you shouldn't be afraid to ask specific questions, but listen for the Holy Spirit's cues and clues as well.

4. **Look for miraculous results**—you should have a positive outcome that you've anticipated. The more you expect God to move, the more this faith posture will be rewarded.

5. **Leave positively**—you should try to end it on a positive note, so the next occasion finds them open for more.

Outtakes Countdowns

10. **Develop confidence based on your value as a child of God.** You mustn't fall into the trap of finding value or confidence in the illusions of success or failure as the world defines it.

9. **Develop the conviction that the same grace that brought salvation is the same grace that will defeat the works of darkness (1 Thessalonians 5:24).** Somebody get on the piano and sing "Amazing Grace." God's grace is multifaceted and is still amazing.

8. **Be convinced that God is in control (Numbers 13:30).** You will succeed with a "we can take the land" attitude. Your activation depends on your having a spirit that follows God fully and trusts Him on the throne completely.

7. **Realize that earthly persecution doesn't diminish your heavenly position.** Read *Foxe's Book of Martyrs* and see how the early saints never lost spiritual altitude over the Neros and other megalomaniacs who thought they could take over.

6. **Just sit back and rehearse in your spirit what God has brought you through (1 Samuel 17:34-37).** By doing this, you will feel up to the task of whatever God calls you to do.

5. **Jesus is looking for you to challenge the authority of those things that conflict with His Word.** Somebody has got to stand against the giant; it might as well be you. David took out his giant, Goliath. Goliath means "heap" and "revolution." David opposed the heap (the lie) and brought back a revolution (Goliath's head) by taking a stand.

4. **You have been deputized to see heaven's blueprint become earth's reality (Matthew 6:10).** Look for daily opportunities to exercise this authority. At any given moment earth's reality could be revolutionized by a simple child of God with the authority of the name of Jesus.

3. **Meditate on the fact that human beings were the original tenants and lease holders to planet earth (Genesis 1:26-28).** For that matter, we're not even going to let the devil have the air without taking back territory.

2. **Be a true ambassador at your marketplace post.** An ambassador enters another land to speak and act on behalf of his own kingdom.

    "In order to operate in the gift of healing, I must be absolutely single-minded, believing in the authority that He has given me in the Word of God."
    – *Bill Subritzky*

1. **Realize in your spirit that overcoming extra opposition leads to receiving extra blessings.** Keep overcoming resistance and opposition in being a prophetic evangelist.

Prophetic Evangelism – Field Activation Manual
Scene Study
Fill In the Blanks

Q. 1. What is God's purpose for working miracles?

_____

_____

_____

_____

Q. 2. The *dunamis* lifestyle is about the _____ of the believer that God has _____ inside of you.

Q. 3. Divine _____ is what furnishes you with supernatural _____.

Q. 4. Spiritual authority consists of what three things?

_____

_____

_____

_____

Q. 5. Authority gives us the _____ to use the _____ God has given us because of our _____ with Him.

Q. 6. How can authority grow in your life?

_____

_____

_____

_____

Extensive Scene Study
Bonus Questions

Q. 1. What is spiritual leverage?

_____

_____

_____

_____

Q. 2. What does the snake becoming a rod of authority in Moses' hand illustrate?

_____

_____

_____

_____

Q. 3. Abstaining from _____ in the face of danger only prolongs the

_____.

Behind the Scenes
Discussion Questions

Discussion Location: Classroom

1. If knowing what Jesus has done for us and who He's made us to be produces a successful ministry, do you have a successful ministry? If not, what is the missing ingredient?

2. *Prophetic Evangelism* states, "I don't want to be satisfied with simply retelling a story of what God did in the past. If all we do is sit back and talk about what other great people have done in the past, we're missing the mark." Talk about what God has done through you in the "now."

3. Revival has a great attraction today. God is glorified in revival, and He puts a DNA in people's spirits during revival. Describe the word revival from your experience.   In your own words, define what revival should be.

4. Gordon Lindsey once said, "Every person called to ministry must decide what their attitude will be toward the supernatural." What is your attitude toward the supernatural?
   a. If God were to speak to you like Moses and say, "What's in your hand?" What would be your answer?
   b. Are you willing to let God use what is in your hand?

5. What does the phrase "spiritual authority" bring to mind when you hear it?

Cutting Room Floor
Application

The shepherd's rod, during the life of Moses, was a journal of past life experiences. When God spoke to Moses and said, "What's in your hand?", Moses said, "A rod." On Moses' rod were carved images of important things that happened in his life. When Moses gave God what was in his hand, it became God's rod instead of Moses' rod.

Using your creativity, go out and find a rod that you can mark so that it tells a story of your life's past experiences, including your testimony and places of growth. This rod can stay in your home or office, as it will provide an open door to share your life story of how God has impacted your life. This rod can illustrate the ongoing story of what God is doing in your life, a symbolic journal of your life's journey.

The Making of an Epic
Journaling

1. Journal about the area or areas in your life where you need to step out so God's spiritual authority in you can grow.

2. Write down some scriptures on authority that have meant the most to you.

Journal Notes

Journal Notes

Chapter 12

The New Face of
Prophetic Evangelism

"The highest and deepest pleasures available to a human being are the
transcendent pleasures that come from personally connecting with God."
– *Michael Sullivant*

Favorite Scene Selections
Sowing into the Divine Function

My favorite scene selection falls in the "Sowing into the Divine Function" segment. Page 207 in *Prophetic Evangelism* states, "Witnessing requires the constant
development of skill, along with nurturing, through prayer and openness to the
Holy Spirit." This is so important to understand because Satan's greatest attack
against Christians who desire to witness is to make you think you should wait until
you are good at witnessing before you witness. Now think about the logic of that
for a moment. Do we make babies sit in their crib until they can walk with perfect equilibrium? Do we make musicians stay off their instrument until they
become virtuosos? No! We must realize that mistakes are not optional in the
learning curve of any worthwhile accomplishment.

"We must not be led astray from the essential work of the Christian ministry by
imagining we have some gift that does not include with it something of the evangelistic necessity, or urging the claim of Christ upon individuals."
– *G. Cambell Morgan*

Jesus told His disciples in Matthew 4:19, "Follow me and I will make you fishers of men." The Greek word for "make" means "to be the authors of a thing, to
fashion and construct," and it implies a designation of time. If you continue to follow the finger of Christ and share your faith, you are being morphed into an effective prophetic evangelist.

**As you expect to be used in prophetic evangelism, you will pick up on more
keys that God will give you in the midstream of conversation with the
unchurched.** You must remember that the more you step out and share your faith,
the more you gather wisdom and skill. Some things we learn by experience, and
some things we learn by watching others. We learn discernment by practice. I'm
convinced that you also possess some gifts that may be dormant but have been
given to you to make you a part of an end-time historic ingathering of souls.

So act like the champion you are. More people act their way into feeling than feel their way into acting! It takes much more effort to begin to move than to change direction.

Director's Bonus Commentary
Prophetic Evangelism: Not a Cookie-Cutter Affair

"God uses all kinds of tomb raiders."
– *Winkie Pratney*

"Because of the empowering of the Holy Spirit, a people will emerge from the shadows of a fearful Christian witness into a free, bold expression of the life of Jesus within them. Some will focus on the words, some on acts of mercy, some on prayer, and some on lifestyle. But through each one the Holy Spirit will work out His divine purposes."
– *Clive Calver*

I can remember years ago coming across a book on soul winning that talked about different types of evangelism. Prophetic evangelism includes power evangelism, servant evangelism, contact evangelism, friendship evangelism, open-air evangelism, prayer evangelism, and so on! It all depends on what the Holy Spirit is breathing on.

Here are some biblical examples of diverse expressions of evangelism.

1. Invitational evangelism (2 Kings 5 1-6). A servant girl connected Naaman to the man of God, Elisha, who released a redemptive command of healing over Naaman's leprosy. This type of evangelism involves connecting with an individual and inviting him out to an encounter opportunity in order to get saved.

2. *Koinonia*—hospitality evangelism (Luke 5:29). Matthew, also called Levi, invited many of his friends to his house for a feast, and Jesus came and talked to them. *Koinonia* is a Greek word that means partnership, participation, and communion. Hospitality is seen when we have a personal gathering with the unchurched and bring in redemptive influences to get them a witness.

3. Power-healing evangelism (John 9, Acts 3, Luke 18: 38-39). Power-healing evangelism usually involves a healing, miracle, or signs that arrest attention followed by someone preaching the Word.

4. Presence evangelism (2 Chronicles 29). King Hezekiah became a lightning rod for God by going after God's presence. The people just kept coming to get right with God. We see this type of evangelism in special meetings, certain areas, and particular vessels in which God has especially touched.

5. Open-air evangelism (Acts 2: 14-41). Peter stood up on the day of Pentecost and preached the gospel to those who had gathered. This happens on college campuses, in the city squares, and at special outdoor events or outreaches.

6. Apologetics evangelism (Acts 17: 17-34). Paul reasoned with the synagogue Jews and used a reasoned argument appeal with the men of Athens. This can be seen in intellectual approaches to rational appeals.

7. Power-encounter evangelism (Acts 8:4-13; Acts 16:16-31). Phillip confronted the bewitching spells of Simon the sorcerer by preaching Christ and destroying the works of darkness. Paul cast out the devil and dropped the psychic hotline of his day off of the air. God may use you in deliverance over a soul who is bound, or you may be directed to break a deceptive addiction off of someone's life.

8. Servant evangelism (Acts 9:36). Dorcas was full of charitable deeds and was obviously influential in the early church. This is seen in adopt-the-block, service-oriented programs like making cookies for a neighbor, helping out single moms, and so on.

9. Contact evangelism (Acts 19:21-27, John 4). Jesus walked up to a stranger for the purpose of leading her to truth. Paul talked to people he had never encountered before about the true God. This can be seen in canvassing-style evangelism in which you walk up to strangers and engage them in redemptive conversation.

10. Situational evangelism/divine appointment (Acts 16: 25-30). Paul seized the opportunity to share hope at a time when the Philippian jailer was desperate. You might be led into a situation or find an individual who is desperate for what Jesus alone can bring him; you then find that he is ripe for harvesting.

11. Friendship evangelism (Luke 19: 5-10, John 4:39). Jesus became friends with Zacchaeus and went over to his house, witnessed to him, and saw him repent. Many times God leads you into redemptive relationships to allow you to shine your light up close, and share your life message with others.

12. Crusade evangelism (John 4:40-41, Matthew 5). Many times Jesus spoke before large crowds who hadn't come to the knowledge of Him. He did it to show them the way to the Father. Both at home and abroad, many people get saved through large-scale meetings.

Remember realism is your friend; you've got to be yourself. God made you unique for a unique assignment in the new millennium that I believe will culminate in the greatest awakening the world has ever seen.

Deleted Footage
Extreme Effective Invitations

Today many churches and Christians no longer plead for a response from the seeker. Several reasons are cited for this, yet the gospel demands a response. We don't want to abort their discovery process, yet many unbelievers don't understand repentance, commitment, and future evangelism without signing their name on the bottom line of God's covenant.

In Exodus 32:26, Moses asked people to make a quality decision as to whose side they were on; they had to cross the line. Joshua, in Joshua 24:15, told people to "choose for yourselves this day whom you will serve." Elijah told a crowd of people that they could not stall in indecision; they had to follow one master alone (1 Kings 18:21).

In the book of Acts, we're told that 3,000 got saved on the day of Pentecost (Acts 2:41). Another 5,000 got saved soon after (Acts 4:4). Alan Street rightly says, "For converts to be accountable, they had to be identifiable. There had to be some means of distinguishing the saved from the lost." What Street means is that those book of Acts converts had to have responded to some invitation. We are fishers of men, and no fisherman throws in a net without bringing it back in. God is going to anoint you afresh to uniquely bring the net in.

I've heard that the great Billy Graham does not prepare his invitation in advance; he extends them extemporaneously (extemporaneous means unrehearsed and spontaneous), being led by the Spirit. You and I can learn from one of the most successful evangelists of our time. Be in the moment; be led by the Spirit in giving an invitation for people to get saved.

We are FISHERS OF MEN, *and no fisherman throws in a net without* BRINGING IT BACK IN. Billy Graham has said that when he gives his final invitation and its time for the people to respond, he experiences extreme warfare. He has said, "I cannot tell you the pressure I experience within. Suddenly I am made aware of the forces of evil and the forces of good, which are fighting for men's souls." Billy Graham also experiences doubts and intense feelings. You must know that hell hates for you to call for a quality decision, which is a clue as to how imperative it is that you go there and close the deal. I have found that if we make our final appeal personal and prophetic, the hearers will feel that it speaks directly to them.

D.L. Moody, the great evangelist, said that the greatest blunder of his ministry was when he failed to give an invitational appeal to lost people. He allowed them to think it over, giving them until next Sunday to respond. During that timeframe, the great Chicago fire broke out killing hundreds and leaving 90,000 people homeless.

Moody would later say, "I have hard work to keep back the tears today.... One lesson I learned that night which I have never forgotten, and that is when I preach, to press Christ upon the people then and there and try to bring them to a decision on the spot. I would rather have the right hand cut off than to give an audience now a week to decide what to do with Jesus." Remember, not everybody will return to that place, room, or situation. Nondecision is not a gospel option. You can't cater to that without regretting it at some later point.

Our mission as prophetic evangelists is to reproduce, as faithfully as possible, the New Testament emphasis; to live out the vintage book of Acts standard. You will never be the same as you undertake this sacred trust.

Alternate Endings
No More Labor Shortages

The first W.A.T.T. of this chapter is that you are called to bear fruit, much fruit for that matter (John 15:16). Jesus calls you to be the leaven that fills the whole loaf (Matthew 13:33), and you're part of the "cut out stone," which grows and becomes a great mountain and fills the earth (Daniel 1:34-35). Quite simply, God has increase on His mind and spiritual growth on His heart. So you can't afford to be complacent or take the attitude that you've arrived either qualitatively or quantitatively. Jesus has a vision of growth and fruit, and you're a major part of that vision (Colossians 1:10).

According to George Barna, we've had an eleven percent drop in seven years in adult attendance in church services. He also found that the number of Christians sharing their faith also declined during that span. It's obvious that there is a correlation between the two stats. Bottom line, whenever the church turns inward, it goes comatose, flat-lined, it dies. When Christians cease to go public with commitment to growth, we concede territory.

In John 4:35-36, Jesus told his followers to "gather fruit for eternal life." He let you in on His motivation and what He burned with. **Your success depends on**

whether we penetrate subcultures or become one. If we allow the devil to downsize our vision to a stained-glass window-shopping Christianity by turning inward, we'll collapse into a subculture that modern culture can easily dismiss. You must come to grips with the fact that Jesus has no plan B to save your city; you're His weapon, strategy, and chief spokesperson. That means He has confidence that Christ in you, the hope of glory, can and will meet the challenge.

Jesus highlighted our last W.A.T.T. in Matthew 9:37-38 by emphasizing that because there's such a massive harvest compared to so few laborers, we have got to see a labor force commensurate, or match up with the harvest. Now there's a difference between busyness and fruitfulness. Busyness is a dangerous diversion of the soul; it lulls you into a false sense of accomplishment. High-impact ministry is not only being fruitful in the off-season (Jeremiah 17:7-8), but it labors to see the release of other laborers. We have taught the priesthood of all believers, but we have not taught the ministry of all believers.

God is coming with a sovereign wave to mobilize an army of prophetic evangelists. The most crucial time in a new believer's life is the first year, just as in a baby's life. Just as so much is set in stone those first four years of life, so are the newborn believer's patterns shaped early on. Your assignment, should you take it, is to take up the mantle of a prophetic evangelist and throw that mantle on as many believers around you as you possibly can. Start your own prophetic evangelism equipping study. If they're not equipped, they will be whipped.

Jesus's statement, "the harvest is plentiful, but the laborers are few" is a mathematic ratio that is true over any city or campus. Show me all the willing laborers and there are always few in proportion to the plentiful mass of folks ripe to be saved. There will always be more fish than fishermen. Remember, you are in it to win it for fruit that remains!

Outtakes Countdown

10. **Get smarter by teaching others.** You can only keep what you give away. The way to grow in any revelation is to share the concept with others, and as you do the Holy Spirit adds to your understanding while causing you to be more fluent in your grasp of the idea and insight. It's been said that "when the student is ready, the teacher will appear," but I submit to you, when the teacher (you) is ready, the students (others) will appear.

You will help your cause if you make sure you are certain on the essentials of salvation. Study various passages in Acts when people are confronted with the gospel. Any time you touch someone else's life, you are setting off a chain reaction that may never end. So take this message from the guttermost to the uttermost.

9. **Use your testimony.** Your testimony is one of the only things that God has given you that can't be conquered or contested. You have a greater anointing to speak on what God has manifested in you. When you speak what God has done in you, it prophetically releases this same miracle in others. Plus you have tip-toe expectation and excitement in that area. Remember that popularity is a line of credit that you can use to tell the truth.

8. **Look to soar with your strengths.** Effective, successful people don't waste their time limping with their weakness, but they soar with their strengths. Are you humorous or are you logical? Are you a good storyteller or a street rapper for Jesus? Whatever it is, use it all for the glory of God. Take a few minutes from time to time to quietly list your personal qualities and your past successes and God achievements and review them consistently. You have been called out to use your gifts (Romans 12:6). The only limiting factor is your faith, which will grow each time you soar.

Additional thoughts on strength: 1) Strengths develop within the framework of a mission; never lose sight of the Savior's mission. 2) Strengths develop only in relation to another human being. God will always direct you to help somebody in order to build you up in giftings.

7. **Get rid of what negates your attractiveness (Hebrews 12:1).** When you drop the weight of what holds you back, you'll see passion released in your soul and favor released in their souls for you. When an ordinary person is filled with a righteous passion and favor, the gates of hell tremble. When this happens, an ordinary person ceases to be ordinary. God promises that "His glory will arise upon you" and the nations will be drawn to your brightness (Isaiah 60:1-3). Your key will be to take your light out from under any baskets (Matthew 5:14-15). Caring is so contagious, but so is apathy, so learn not to react with criticism towards the world God has placed you in.

6. **Remember to be on their turf and in their terms.** People need to see someone else step out from the crowd, and then they will receive a shove to step out as well. Being a prophetic evangelist means being a bridge. If a structure doesn't connect to the other side, it is not a bridge. Jesus never waited for the lost to come to Him or speak to them in foreign terms (unless they were Pharisees). He always related to them. Remember that your language makes a

powerful impact on others. If you are going to influence others, you must speak their language.

5. **Seek to remind yourself of who Jesus is and what He told you to do.** Satan loves to hold a counterfeit image before you and put voices of counterfeit authorities in your ear. You must obey God by truly following Him and "speak the things that you see with the Father" (John 8:38). As you hold heaven's internal photograph before you, you will walk as Jesus walked. By doing this your mind will be unfettered because it will be fixed on spiritual things, and your thoughts will empower you.

4. **Be emptied to be filled.** I always make it a point before I minister to empty myself of all "self" inhibitors such as self-reliance, selfish ambition, self-exaltation, and self-glorification. The more you can be emptied, the more the Lord can fill you. You also must empty yourself of preconceived notions of how you will handle witnessing opportunities. Evangelist Scott Hinkle says, "you must lose the Mapquest mentality" where you want it all planned out. You must move on a *mashach* (Hebrew for the word "anointing") mentality, where you seek to allow God's anointing to teach you and lead you.

3. **Avoid presumption and preconceptions.** No two cases or situations are alike. The Mapquest mentality only serves to restrict your effectiveness and negate God's spontaneous downloads or words of knowledge as the moment demands. You need God's FAA. Prophecy, which is impeded by preconceived notions, provides data for your next level of **F**avor, **A**uthority, and **A**nointing (FAA). The gift of a word of knowledge represents the capacity to receive supernaturally revealed knowledge that otherwise could not be known.
This gift of a word of knowledge comes in several stages:
a. The realization that God can and does reveal knowledge
directly to people.
b. The recognition that God is doing it to you (increasing awareness of certain promptings).
c. The conviction that the Holy Spirit wants you to share with others what you have been given.
d. The next level of fluency in the gift is when you see greater frequency and accuracy.
e. An increased liberty to flow in various settings with confidence (open air, marketplaces, etc.).

God can speed these stages up and often with prophetic evangelists.

2. Get honest with the Lord and acknowledge your need of His strength.
Those who do this will taste of the powers of the age to come (Hebrews 6:5). I'm convinced that God will trailblaze a fresh expression of miracles following His message of redemption. It's now time for you to press in for His anointing. You've got to be bold; you can't be afraid of failure. Only those who risk failure will conquer failure. You've got to stand up and stand out to rescue the perishing (Proverbs 24:11).

1. Identify "well" opportunities.
Well opportunities could be areas:
a. Where modern culture fails to provide an answer.
b. Where God has given you a profound grace.
c. Never addressed or challenged in the eyes of the nonchurched.

A well opportunity forces you to differentiate between an activity and an outcome. An outcome is a result and is a quantifiable instance that someone else can verify, whereas an activity is an action that is well-intentioned but is only an interim step towards a result. You must have outcomes in mind concerning well opportunities (i.e., praying with someone or inviting them to take the next step).

In Luke 22:32, Jesus told Peter "when you have returned (Greek word *epistrepho*) to me, strengthen your brethren." *Epistrepho* is a complete turnaround from ignorance and error to true service of God. Now that you have embraced the primary purpose of prophetic evangelism, you must also turn and encourage others in the work of converting sinners to Jesus Christ.

Prophetic Evangelism – Field Activation Manual
Scene Study
Fill In the Blanks

Q. 1. Prophetic evangelism is_____ what God is doing and then _____Him.

Q. 2. What are the 12 principles of the Jesus Style?
   a. Break the _____pattern.
   b. Sense the where or what, before the_____.
   c. Begin where people_____.
   d. Can the _____approach.
   e. Trust the _____that is on you.
   f. Cultivate spiritual _____in others.
   g. Know when to _____up, know when to_____ up.
   h. Keep the _____on focus.
   i. Put their _____back on.
   j. Do_____, love_____.
   k. Recognize that _____is a divine process.
   l. Recapture the _____and retell the_____.

Extensive Scene Study
Bonus Questions

Q. 1. Outside of the Spirit of Christ, what is the greatest gift we have in this hour?

_____

_____

_____

_____

Q. 2. What you_____, you put in _____.

Q. 3. How is evangelism an art?

_____

_____

_____

_____

Q. 4. _____is not something we do to people; it's something we do with the _____.

Behind the Scenes
Discussion Questions

1. The scripture says, "What He sees the Father do, the Son can do." *Prophetic Evangelism* describes how the Holy Spirit brings all things to your remembrance. It also states that the Holy Spirit actually puts things in your mind. More important, we have access to the mind of Christ. How does having the mind of Christ benefit evangelism?

2. Do you believe that prophetic evangelism will draw you to places before people even get there? Why?

3. Communication is key in prophetic evangelism. How can you learn to communicate the gospel and your testimony in ways that are relevant to our culture today?

4. In *Prophetic Evangelism* we read the statement, "I can go into a witnessing situation with confidence because I know that the Father is going to speak through me. God is going to give you something to say! He cares about the lost way too much to leave them that way." He's not sending us out there to fail; He's sending us out there to be effective. Discuss how confidence has grown in you as you witness.

5. Witnessing requires a constant development of skill. Like any other art, witnessing is an art that you practice and continually work at to become better. What are some ways to practice witnessing that will make you become better?

6. Jesus was an expert at cultivating people's hearts. Using the skills of listening to people's hurts and problems can make your witness strong. How do you balance listening and speaking in witnessing?

7. What are the signs that a person is receptive to your message? Can you think of any people in your life who have shown any of these signs?

Cutting Room Floor
Application

"The word of God tells us to do justice and love mercy. It does not say to love justice and do mercy."
– *Sean Smith*, **Prophetic Evangelism**

Three concerns we always hear people talk about are:
1. Broken homes
2. Prisons
3. Victims

The statement "People get what they deserve" is common in our society. We love to see people in court like Michael Jackson; we love to see justice being served such as in the case of Scott Peterson. We love justice as Christians; we are also called to show mercy.

Task options:
1. Write a letter to some victims of crimes in your community (crisis center, etc.).
2. Write a letter to someone in prison telling him or her about the gospel message (detention centers, etc.).
3. Help a family whose home is broken apart through divorce or other pains that plague our society (your neighborhood, etc.).

Complete two of these tasks. Then come back and present to the group what you have sent, written, and done.

The Making of an Epic
Journaling

1. Jesus always maintained the dignity of the lost when he addressed them. What do you need to put in your life and what do you need to take out of your life to show the same love that Jesus showed? For example, Mother Theresa dealt with the "grostesquely" sick. She had to see each person as being Christ Himself, and then she could get beyond the intensity of the leprosy. This is your opportunity to create a list of what you need to add to your life, or take away from your life, for this to happen.

2. What ways can you influence other believers to become prophetic evangelists?

Journal Notes

Journal Notes

Journal Notes

Journal Notes